VHDL
FOR DIGITAL DESIGN

BICENTENNIAL **1807** **⊛WILEY** **2007** **BICENTENNIAL**

THE WILEY BICENTENNIAL—KNOWLEDGE FOR GENERATIONS

*E*ach generation has its unique needs and aspirations. When Charles Wiley first opened his small printing shop in lower Manhattan in 1807, it was a generation of boundless potential searching for an identity. And we were there, helping to define a new American literary tradition. Over half a century later, in the midst of the Second Industrial Revolution, it was a generation focused on building the future. Once again, we were there, supplying the critical scientific, technical, and engineering knowledge that helped frame the world. Throughout the 20th Century, and into the new millennium, nations began to reach out beyond their own borders and a new international community was born. Wiley was there, expanding its operations around the world to enable a global exchange of ideas, opinions, and know-how.

For 200 years, Wiley has been an integral part of each generation's journey, enabling the flow of information and understanding necessary to meet their needs and fulfill their aspirations. Today, bold new technologies are changing the way we live and learn. Wiley will be there, providing you the must-have knowledge you need to imagine new worlds, new possibilities, and new opportunities.

Generations come and go, but you can always count on Wiley to provide you the knowledge you need, when and where you need it!

WILLIAM J. PESCE
PRESIDENT AND CHIEF EXECUTIVE OFFICER

PETER BOOTH WILEY
CHAIRMAN OF THE BOARD

VHDL
FOR DIGITAL DESIGN

Frank Vahid
University of California, Riverside

Roman Lysecky
University of Arizona

BICENTENNIAL

1807

WILEY

2007

BICENTENNIAL

EXECUTIVE PUBLISHER	Don Fowley
ASSOCIATE PUBLISHER	Dan Sayre
SENIOR ACQUISITIONS EDITOR	Catherine Fields Shultz
PROJECT EDITOR	Gladys Soto
EDITORIAL ASSISTANT	Chelsee Pengal
SENIOR PRODUCTION EDITOR	Ken Santor
COVER DESIGNER	Michael St. Martine

This book was set in Microsoft Word® by the author and printed and bound by Malloy Inc. The cover was printed by Malloy Inc.

This book is printed on acid free paper. ∞

ISBN-13 978-0-470-05263-1

Printed in the United States of America

10 9 8 7 6 5 4 3 2 1

To my family, Amy, Eric, Kelsi, and Maya. — FV

To my father, Gregory. — RL

Preface

TO THOSE ABOUT TO STUDY VHDL

Designing computing systems, which have impacted nearly every aspect of modern life, can be an exciting and rewarding endeavor. The approach to designing the digital circuits underlying those computing systems, a task known as digital design, has seen a major paradigm shift during the past decades. The previous approach of drawing a circuit's interconnection of components has been largely replaced by an approach of describing such circuits in a hardware description language (HDL), and even by an approach of just describing the desired behavior of such circuits in an HDL and letting tools automatically generate the circuits. The net result is that while designer productivity in the early 1980s was about 100-transistors per month, designer productivity in the 2000s exceeds 10,000 transistors per month and is continuing to increase.

In past decades, digital design was used to create microprocessors, and to create the small "glue logic" circuits that allowed microprocessors and other components to interact with surrounding components. While those uses are still common today, digital design has grown to also include creation of high-performance custom circuit implementations of complex digital processing systems, such as modems, network routers and switches, wireless encrypters, and more. Even computations traditionally executed on microprocessors are increasingly migrating to "coprocessor" or "accelerator" digital circuits that enable high-performance applications previously not possible, such as circuits that perform real-time three-dimensional graphics rendering, decode compressed video streams for cell phone video displays, perform real-time speech understanding or face recognition, or analyze huge amounts of biological data in hours rather than months. Such circuits can also result in low power, small size, and/or decreased costs, depending on the application.

In short, digital design is an exciting and important field of study, and HDLs form the the basis of modern digital design. Learning an HDL can thus prove a worthwhile endeavor. VHDL is one of the most widely-used HDLs. Even if one will later use a different HDL, once having learned VHDL, learning other HDLs requires only a fraction of the time, as many basic concepts are similar across different HDLs.

TO TEACHERS OF VHDL

Teachers may note that this book differs somewhat from traditional HDL books—the book emphasizes *design* rather than language. Traditional books are organized by language constructs, perhaps introducing data types, then object declarations, then processes and process statements, etc. This book is instead organized by design concepts, starting with combinational design, then basic sequential design, then datapath component design, and

and finally, register-transfer level design (even touching on algorithmic-level design). The book introduces language constructs as they are needed, being careful to ensure that the most important constructs are covered at some point. The design-based approach may prove more intuitive to students and hence useful to the learning process. The book does contain a mini-reference in the last chapter so that the book can also serve as a reasonable reference for the most important constructs of the language.

The book also clearly distinguishes design (i.e., synthesis) concepts from simulation concepts. This distinction is critical to proper use of an HDL for design, and ultimately it is the design purpose of an HDL that is typically of primary interest when an HDL is being learned.

This book was created with two key uses in mind. One use is in a digital design course as a supplement to a digital design textbook. For that use, the book provides a more thorough introduction to HDL concepts than is possible when HDL concepts are instead contained inside a digital design textbook. The authors do not believe that any existing digital design textbook with integrated HDL coverage provides a sufficient introduction to HDLs. A sufficient HDL introduction—which covers different design abstraction levels, including structural and behavioral design, synthesis concepts, simulation concepts, test-bench concepts, and more—requires about 150–200 pages, which would overly-enlarge most digital design textbooks. (Furthermore, the authors believe that the student is best served by a digital design book that has the student learn key concepts using the most intu-itive means, such as using circuits, truth tables, and state diagrams, before introducing another layer of indirection present in HDLs). Likewise, the authors have found that stan-dalone HDL books having 300–600 pages are too lengthy, detailed, and costly for effec-tive use as a supplement in a digital design course. A few short (200–250 page) introductory HDL books do exist, but we have found them to be language-oriented rather than design oriented. Language-orientation leads to the common situation of students writ-ing HDL code that simulates fine, and then expressing frustration and bewilderment when that code does not synthesize correctly. While this book can be used as a supplement to any digital design textbook, it ideally supplements the textbook *Digital Design* by Frank Vahid (John Wiley and Sons, Inc.), following the same chapter structure, using the same terminology, and using many of the same examples.

The second use of this book is as a standalone HDL introduction. The authors believe that the concepts covered are ideally suited as an introduction, enough to enable design of combinational logic, sequential logic, datapath components, and register-transfer level designs, but not so much as to overwhelm the reader with advanced constructs. As such, this book may serve well in a first course on HDL-based design, which is typically an upper-division undergraduate or even graduate level course. A second course on HDL-based design might use a lengthier HDL book.

ABOUT THE BOOK

CHAPTER OVERVIEW

This book is about digital design using an HDL. Its chapters cover increasingly complex digital design concepts and introduces HDL constructs as they are needed. After an intro-duction to HDL-based design in Chapter 1, Chapter 2 discusses basic combinational logic design, and Chapter 3 discusses basic sequential logic design. Chapter 4 introduces the design of some common datapath components, such that other datapath components could easily be described using similar techniques. Chapter 5 introduces register-transfer level (RTL) design, the design level at which the majority of digital designs are described in HDLs today. Finally, Chapter 6 provides a mini-reference to the most common HDL constructs. Most of those constructs were introduced in the earlier chapters, but Chapter 6 provides a handy means for quickly looking up the key aspects of each language construct, as well as serving as a good review after reading the earlier chapters. Chapter 6 also provides coverage of a few advanced constructs that are often useful for larger HDL designs.

Because the same HDL is typically used for both design (synthesis) purposes and for purely simulation purposes (as in a testbench for testing a design), subsections that deal specifically with synthesis or with simulation are noted as such using special icons next to the subsection headings, namely with ⎮ for synthesis and with ⊓⊔⊓ for simulation.

ACCOMPANYING RESOURCES

This book contains several accompanying resources and related items.

All HDL code in the text comes from complete VHDL files that have been compiled and simulated with a commercial VHDL simulator, and that code is available to users of this book.

The book comes with a complete set of graphical, carefully-colored, animated Power-Point slides. Every figure in the book comes from a figure in the slides. The slides may prove very useful to the reader as a learning tool—readers may in fact find that a good approach to learning the HDL is to first progress through the animated slides, and then refer to the book for a more in-depth explanation. Teachers may find that the slides serve as a truly useful teaching tool. It might interest teachers to know that the authors actually developed the slides first, before writing the book itself—the authors consider the slides as a critical part of the complete teaching package, rather than as an afterthought.

A 550-page introductory digital design textbook whose chapters and examples largely match those in this book is available for in-depth study of the digital design concepts in this book.

A matching book that has the same structure and examples but that introduces the Verilog language is also available.

HDLs are best learned through experience, and thus readers are strongly encouraged to actively use a VHDL simulator while learning the material in this book. Fortunately, free or low-cost versions of several high-quality commercial simulators have become available in recent years.

Information on the above resources and items can be found at the book's website, reachable from the site: *http://www.ddvahid.com*.

FORMATTING

The code that appears in the text has been cut-and-pasted directly from tested HDL files. Thus, one may note that the formatting of the HDL code is not as "pretty" as in many other HDL books, which may bold or color HDL keywords in their code samples. However, the authors felt that correctness of the code outweighed any benefits gained from bolded or colored code, which would have required manual retyping or modification of the tested code, and which often explains the subtle mistakes commonly found in the code of many HDL books. Therefore, the book uses the convention of typing HDL keywords in all capital letters (e.g., PROCESS). That convention allowed for the cut-and-paste method of including code in the book, while still clearly distinguishing HDL keywords from user-created identifiers in the code. The authors point out, however, that HDL coders typically do not use the capitalized-keyword convention, as most HDL-entry tools automatically bold or color the keywords for a designer.

The text in this book intentionally violates the basic English punctuation rule of placing sentence punctuation within quoted text, such as the final period in the quoted text: "Hello." In this book, such text would appear as: "Hello". For normal English, the punctuation rule is a bit inelegant (at least to us computer-language types), but when quoting HDL code, the rule could cause great confusion. HDL code samples in this book will thus be shown as follows: "$x <= $ "00";". The alternative, with sentence punctuation within the quotes, could have confused the reader into thinking that the sentence punctuation is part of the HDL code, as in: "$x <= $ "00";." In that code example, a reader may think that the period is part of the HDL code.

ACKNOWLEDGMENTS

We would like to thank John Wiley and Sons publishers, and in particular Gladys Soto and Catherine Shultz, for their support of this book. We are also grateful to David Sheldon, Greg Stitt, Scott Sirowy, and Ann Gordon-Ross, for their assistance in proofreading and checking various HDL code samples. We thank Brian Alleyne of Cisco Systems for his helpful input, and we thank the many engineers from Intel, IBM, Motorola, Freescale, and Xilinx, with whom we have worked during the years and who have in one way or another contributed to the concepts in this book. The research support from the National Science Foundation has also been instrumental in providing a solid foundation for the authors and is thus acknowledged with sincere gratitude.

ABOUT THE AUTHORS

Frank Vahid is a Professor of Computer Science and Engineering at the University of California, Riverside, and is the Associate Director of the Center for Embedded Computer Systems at the University of California, Irvine. He received his B.S. in Computer Engineering from the University of Illinois in 1988, and his M.S. and Ph.D. in Computer Science from the University of California, Irvine in 1990 and 1994, respectively. He has taught, researched, worked, and consulted in the field of digital design since 1986. His experience with HDLs includes not only writing a VHDL compiler and developing numerous HDL-based synthesis tools, but also includes writing many thousands of lines of HDL code for synthesis. He has authored the textbooks "Specification and Design of Embedded Systems (Prentice-Hall, 1994), "Embedded System Design: A Unified Hardware/Software Introduction" (John Wiley and Sons, 2001), and "Digital Design" (John Wiley and Sons, 2007). He has published over 150 research papers, chaired major symposia in the field of embedded system design (including ISSS and CODES), held engineering positions at Hewlett Packard and AMCC, consulted for numerous companies including Motorola and NEC, holds several U.S. patents, and conducts collaborative digital design research with several companies including Intel, IBM, Freescale, and Xilinx.

Roman Lysecky is an Assistant Professor of Electrical and Computer Engineering at the University of Arizona. He received his B.S., M.S., and Ph.D. in Computer Science from the University of California, Riverside in 1999, 2000, and 2005, respectively. His expertise in HDLs and synthesis of digital designs includes writing tens of thousands of lines of synthesizable HDL code, including several microprocessor designs, a high-performance profiler, dozens of hardware coprocessors for multimedia, automotive, and digital signal processing applications, a multi-channel DMA controller, as well as a custom FPGA design, all synthesized as ASIC or FPGA circuits. He has extensive experience with simulation and synthesis tools from Synopsys, Cadence, Mentor Graphics, Aldec, and Xilinx, including synthesizing a custom FPGA design, described using an HDL, as a 0.13μm circuit, simulated and verified at the post-layout level in collaboration with Intel. He has developed several computer-aided design tools for ASICs and FPGAs, including logic synthesis, technology mapping, and place and route tools. He has published many research papers, receiving the Best Paper Award at the Design Automation and Test in Europe Conference (DATE), and holds one U.S. patent.

Contents

CHAPTER 1

Introduction

1.1 DIGITAL SYSTEMS

Digital systems surround us, being present in almost any modern device that uses electricity. A ***digital system*** is an electronic system that operates on two-valued electric signals, referred to as *'1'* and *'0'*. The most common implementation of digital systems today is on an ***integrated circuit***, or IC, also known as a "chip." Figure 1.1 shows an IC package whose cover had been removed, revealing the normally-hidden IC inside, surrounded by the package's pins that connect to the IC's perimeter.

Figure 1.1 An integrated circuit (IC).

The most widely-known digital systems are computers, such as desktop computers ("PCs") and laptop computers, shown in Figure 1.2(a). However, digital systems appear inside a multitude of other devices, such as those in Figure 1.2(b), including:

- Consumer electronics: Cell phones, portable music players, cameras, video game consoles, electronic music instruments, etc.

- Medical equipment: Hearing aids, pacemakers, life support systems, etc.

      (a)   **(b)**

Figure 1.2 Digital system examples: (a) computers, (b) diverse electronic devices.

- Automotive electronics: Engine control, anti-lock brakes, navigation systems, cruise controllers, etc.
- And much more: Military equipment, networking equipment, office electronics, etc.

Such digital systems, which are embedded within larger electronic devices, are often referred to as *embedded systems*.

1.2 HARDWARE DESCRIPTION LANGUAGES

Digital systems have become increasingly complex during the past several decades. This increase in complexity is due to what is known as Moore's Law—the trend of ICs doubling their capacity to hold digital components (i.e., transistors) roughly every 18 months, illustrated in Figure 1.3. In the 1960s and 1970s, typical ICs might have contained tens to thousands of transistors. In the 1980s, capacities increased to the hundreds of thousands. The 1990s saw capacities in the tens of millions. ICs of the 2000s reached into the billions of transistors per IC.

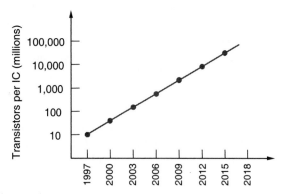

Figure 1.3 IC capacities have doubled roughly every 18 months (Moore's Law), leading to increasingly complex ICs.

In the 1970s, after an IC was built, the IC's behavior would be documented through a combination of schematics (circuit drawings), diagrams, and natural language (such as English) descriptions, as illustrated in Figure 1.4. The size of such documentation commonly reached hundreds of pages. Engineers that purchased ICs to use in their own systems would have to read that documentation to understand the behavior of the ICs, so that those engineers could properly design other systems that interfaced with the ICs. However, reading hundreds of pages of documentation was hard. Furthermore, that documentation often contained errors and ambiguities. Engineers using ICs thus often had trouble integrating those ICs with other ICs, and with other devices in their systems.

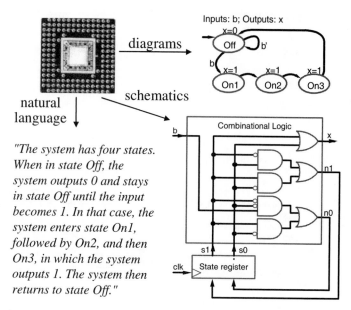

Figure 1.4 ICs of the 1970s were documented using schematics, diagrams, and natural language descriptions, resulting in hundreds of pages of documentation.

Frustrated with this situation, the U.S. Department of Defense (DoD) sought a method by which IC providers could precisely describe the behavior of their ICs. The DoD thus initiated development of a hardware description language. A *hardware description language*, or **HDL**, is a machine-readable and human-readable textual language for describing hardware. An HDL is precise and can thus be automatically simulated to see exactly how an IC is supposed to behave. *Simulation* is a procedure wherein a tool, known as a simulator, automatically generates output values of a hardware module for a given sequence of input values. Figure 1.5 illustrates how an HDL could be used to describe the behavior of an IC, and then simulated to create output values for given input values

The HDL that the U.S. DoD created in the 1980s is called VHDL. **VHDL** stands for the **V**HSIC **H**ardware **D**escription **L**anguage. *VHSIC* itself stands for *Very High Speed Integrated Circuit*, which was a project of the DoD. The DoD assembled a group of people with different backgrounds and from different companies to define the language. VHDL was defined to have a syntax very similar to the Ada language, a software programming language whose development was also spurred by the DoD in the late 1970s. In 1987, the Institute of Electrical and Electronics Engineers, or IEEE, adopted VHDL as standard number 1076. Having VHDL become an IEEE standard meant that companies creating VHDL simulators would (in principle) have a single clear language definition to support, rather than having to try to support the many language variations that would have otherwise likely evolved in the absence of a standard.

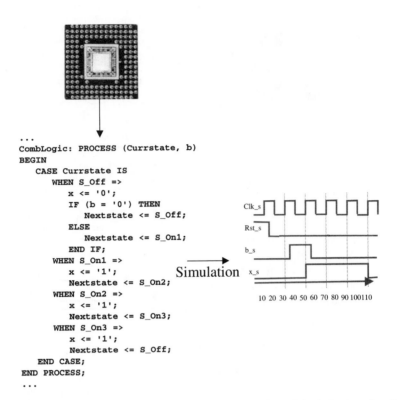

```
...
CombLogic: PROCESS (Currstate, b)
BEGIN
   CASE Currstate IS
      WHEN S_Off =>
         x <= '0';
         IF (b = '0') THEN
            Nextstate <= S_Off;
         ELSE
            Nextstate <= S_On1;
         END IF;
      WHEN S_On1 =>
         x <= '1';
         Nextstate <= S_On2;
      WHEN S_On2 =>
         x <= '1';
         Nextstate <= S_On3;
      WHEN S_On3 =>
         x <= '1';
         Nextstate <= S_Off;
   END CASE;
END PROCESS;
...
```

Figure 1.5 An HDL provides a precise machine-readable description of the behavior of an IC, enabling simulation and hence clear knowledge of how an IC's outputs would react to a given sequence of inputs.

VHDL is one of three popular modern HDLs. A second HDL, Verilog, was also developed in the 1980s, by a particular electronics company. Verilog was developed to have a syntax similar to the C programming language, which was the most popular software programming language in industry in the 1980s. After VHDL became an IEEE standard in 1987, the company that owned Verilog may have realized that Verilog would also have to become a standard in order for the language and its associated tools to adequately compete with the VHDL language and VHDL's evolving commercial tools. Verilog became IEEE standard number 1364 in the year 1995.

A third HDL, SystemC, has recently evolved. The continued capacity increases of ICs resulted in the increasingly common situation of multiple microprocessors and custom hardware circuits co-existing on a single IC. Such system-on-a-chip ICs require integrated simulation of both microprocessor software and custom circuit hardware. Some tools, known as *co-simulators*, evolved in the 1990s seeking to link hardware simulations (using languages like VHDL or Verilog) with microprocessor simulators (executing code written in languages like C or C++). In contrast to such tools, SystemC was developed in the 2000s by several companies seeking to develop a single language suitable for efficiently simulating all of a system's software and hardware components using a single language and simulation envi-

```
ENTITY DoorOpener IS
    PORT (c, h, p: IN std_logic;
          f: OUT std_logic);
END DoorOpener;

ARCHITECTURE Beh OF DoorOpener IS
BEGIN
    PROCESS(c, h, p)
    BEGIN
        f <= NOT(c) AND (h OR p);
    END PROCESS;
END Beh;
```

(a)

```
module DoorOpener(c,h,p,f);
    input c, h, p;
    output f;
    reg f;

    always @(c or h or p)
    begin
        f <= (~c) & (h | p);
    end
endmodule
```

(b)

```
#include "systemc.h"
SC_MODULE(DoorOpener)
{
    sc_in<sc_logic> c, h, p;
    sc_out<sc_logic> f;

    SC_CTOR(DoorOpener)
    {
        SC_METHOD(comblogic);
        sensitive << c << h << p;
    }

    void comblogic()
    {
        f.write((~c.read()) & (h.read() | p.read()));
    }
};
```

(c)

Figure 1.6 HDL descriptions of a simple circuit: (a) VHDL, (b) Verilog, and (c) SystemC.

ronment. SystemC consists of libraries and macro routines added to the popular C++ object-oriented software programming language. As such, some people argue that SystemC is not really a hardware description language, but rather a system description language. SystemC became IEEE standard number 1666 in the year 2005. SystemC is a bit cumbersome for describing low-level hardware, but excels at system-level descriptions.

Figure 1.6 illustrates the description of a simple circuit's behavior in all three languages: VHDL, Verilog, and SystemC.

1.3 HDLS FOR DESIGN AND SYNTHESIS

Although VHDL was originally defined and used primarily as a language for documenting an already-designed IC, the language evolved to be increasingly used for design and synthesis. *Design* in this context refers to converting a higher-level description of a system into a lower-level description representing an implementation. Designers began using HDLs to

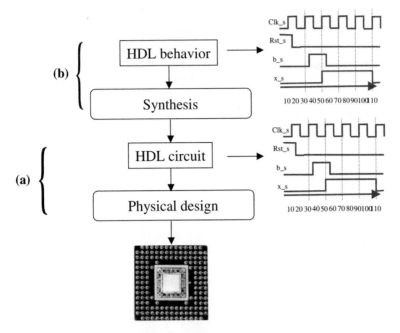

Figure 1.7 Evolution of HDLs as a design and synthesis language, rather than just a documentation language: (a) used to describe a circuit, followed by evolution of physical design tools to convert circuits to IC implementations, (b) used to describe desired behavior, followed by evolution of synthesis tools that automatically convert such behavior to circuits.

describe circuits before those circuits were implemented on ICs, in order to simulate the circuit to ensure correct behavior, as illustrated in Figure 1.7(a). With the common existence of such HDL circuit descriptions, *physical design* tools evolved to automatically convert those HDL descriptions into IC implementations, thus reducing designer effort.

Furthermore, designers increasingly began to use HDLs to describe the intended behavior of circuits before even designing those circuits, as illustrated in Figure 1.7(b). Designers simulated those behavioral descriptions first to ensure correct functionality. Those behavioral descriptions were far simpler than circuit descriptions, allowing the designer to focus on high-level functional concepts ("What should happen if these two inputs both become '1' at the same time?") before dealing with low-level issues ("Should this register be connected to that logic gate?"). Designers then converted the behavioral description into a circuit description, and simulated again—the two simulations should match. **Synthesis tools** evolved to automatically convert behavioral descriptions into circuit descriptions.

This book focuses on the use of VHDL for design (rather than documentation), with a heavy emphasis on the language's use for synthesis. Many people learning VHDL are doing so to be able use synthesis tools, such as tools that map VHDL code onto field-programmable gate array. A *field-programmable gate array (FPGA)* is an increasingly popular type of off-the-shelf IC that can be configured to implement custom circuits merely by programming the IC with a series of bits, akin to programming a microprocessor IC. However, VHDL is a general language intended for documentation and simulation, as well as for synthesis. Therefore, not all VHDL code that simulates can also be synthesized into circuits by synthesis tools. As a simple example, VHDL supports recursively-called functions, but no modern synthesis tool synthesizes circuits for such functions. New VHDL users may write code that simulates correctly, but that does not synthesize to a working circuit. Those users often conclude that the synthesis tools are weak or faulty. While some tools may indeed be weak or faulty, in many cases the problem is that the VHDL code was not reasonably written for synthesis purposes.

As an analogy, consider a natural language like English. On the one hand, English is a very general language, suitable for a variety of purposes including conversation, textbooks, jokes, poetry, and cooking recipes. On the other hand, the specific purpose of cooking recipes involves a highly-specialized use of the language. A reasonable recipe might use words like stir, blend, eggs, and bowl, but would not use words like bludgeon, harmonic, forthright, and castigate. A recipe using such words may represent correct English grammar, but if the food doesn't turn out well, we should not blame the chef.

Likewise, VHDL is a very general language, suitable for a variety of purposes. But when used for synthesis, the language must be used in a disciplined restricted manner.

Many VHDL textbooks introduce the VHDL language first, construct by construct, and then later describe how to use the language for synthesis. However, if one seeks to learn the English language primarily for the purpose of writing recipes in English, learning the entire English language first is not necessarily the best approach. Likewise, if one seeks to learn the VHDL language for the purpose of synthesis, learning the entire VHDL language first is not necessarily the best approach either. Not only would learning the general language involve extraneous information not central to one's purpose, but even the relevant information being learned might be better understood if introduced in the context of the desired purpose—clear motivating examples often enhance learning.

This book therefore differs from many other introductory VHDL books. Rather than being organized around VHDL language constructs, the book is instead organized around increasingly complex digital design tasks: combinational logic design, sequential logic design, datapath component design, and finally register-transfer level (RTL) design. For each design task, the book introduces the VHDL constructs necessary to accomplish those tasks. In summary, the book is designed as an introduction to using VHDL for digital design, rather than as a reference book on the VHDL language. Nevertheless, through use of the mini-reference chapter and the extensive index at the end of the book, this book can also serve as a useful reference book.

This *VHDL for Digital Design* book can be used as a standalone introduction to VHDL. However, this book was also created to be easily used as a supplement to the textbook *Digital Design* by Frank Vahid, published by John Wiley and Sons, Inc. The chapters of this book follow the *Digital Design* textbook's chapter organization, and many of the examples come from that textbook too. A learning of digital design via the *Digital Design* textbook can be supplemented by following the study of each textbook chapter with a study of this book's corresponding chapter, e.g., following *Digital Design* Chapter 2 by this book's Chapter 2, following *Digital Design* Chapter 3 by this book's Chapter 3, and so on for Chapters 4 and 5 too.

The book is organized as follows. Chapter 2 introduces the description in VHDL of basic combinational components. Chapter 3 introduces the description of basic sequential components. Chapter 4 covers description techniques for datapath components, both combinational and sequential. Chapter 5 describes register-transfer level design. Throughout each chapter, VHDL constructs are introduced as they are needed, as are key HDL concepts such as building a testbench, understanding how a simulator works, and debugging. Furthermore, each chapter stresses a top-down design approach, wherein components are first described behaviorally, and then refined into a structural description.

CHAPTER 2

Combinational Logic Design

2.1 *AND*, *OR*, AND *NOT* GATES

AND, OR, and NOT gates are the basic components of digital design. We begin by showing how to define and simulate those gate components.

ENTITIES AND PORTS

Defining a new component in VHDL begins by defining a new design entity. A ***design entity*** is the main hardware abstraction in VHDL, having inputs, outputs, and a well-defined function. A design entity definition consists of two parts.

The first part is an entity declaration, shown in Figure 2.1 for 2-input AND, 2-input OR, and NOT components. An ***entity declaration*** defines the entity's *interface* to the outside world, including the entity's name, and the entity's inputs and outputs. In Figure 2.1, we named the entities *And2*, *Or2*, and *Inv*, respectively. Those names could have been different ones, like *Fred*, *George*, and *Bob*, but the names *And2*, *Or2*, and *Inv* are more descriptive of the items being created.

The entity's inputs and outputs, known as ***ports*** appear in a list contained between the parentheses of the statement "*PORT ( );*". Semicolons separate each port in the list — note that the last port is not followed by a semicolon, since there is no following port from which to separate. Each port consists of a name, a direction (e.g., IN or OUT), and a type. In Figure 2.1, all the ports are of type ***std_logic***, which at this point can be thought of simply as a bit type that can have a value of *'0'* or *'1'*. To save space, multiple ports of the same direction and type could be grouped together, e.g., "*x, y: IN std_logic*".

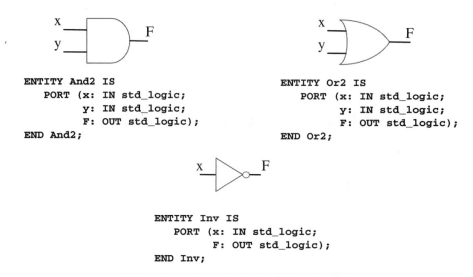

```
ENTITY And2 IS
    PORT (x: IN std_logic;
          y: IN std_logic;
          F: OUT std_logic);
END And2;
```

```
ENTITY Or2 IS
    PORT (x: IN std_logic;
          y: IN std_logic;
          F: OUT std_logic);
END Or2;
```

```
ENTITY Inv IS
    PORT (x: IN std_logic;
          F: OUT std_logic);
END Inv;
```

Figure 2.1 Entity declarations for AND, OR, and NOT (Inv) gates.

The VHDL code in Figure 2.1 consists of several VHDL reserved words and several user-defined names. A ***reserved word*** is an identifier that has special significance in the language and may not be used as a user-defined name. VHDL reserved words appearing in Figure 2.1 are *ENTITY, IS, PORT, IN, OUT*, and *END*. ***User-defined names*** are identifiers used to describe parts of a design. User-defined names appearing in Figure 2.1 are *And2, Or2, Inv, x, y*, and *F*. User-defined names must start with a letter, optionally followed by any sequence of letters, numbers, and underscore characters, with the restrictions that two underscores cannot appear in a row and an underscore cannot be the last character of an identifier. Examples of valid and invalid user-defined names include:

- Valid names: *A, x, Hello, JXYZ, B14, Sig432, Wire_23, Index_counter_1, In1, test_entity*
- Invalid names: *IN* (reserved word), *Wire_* (ends in underscore), *Wire__23* (two underscores in a row), *4x1Mux* (doesn't start with a letter), *_in4* (doesn't start with a letter)

This book will use the convention of writing *reserved words in all upper-case letters*, such as for the word *ENTITY*. However, VHDL is ***case insensitive***, meaning there is no difference between upper and lower-case letters. For example, the identifiers *ENTITY, entity, Entity*, and even *EnTiTy*, all have exactly the same meaning. Likewise, the identifiers *And2, and2*, and *AND2* all have the same meaning. Most VHDL editors will automatically bold or color reserved words, eliminating the benefit of making reserved words upper-case. However, for the VHDL shown in this book, we use upper-case to ensure clarity.

Example 2.1: Entity declaration for a 4x1 multiplexor

A 4x1 mux has four data inputs, two select inputs, and a data output. We can name them *i3*, *i2*, *i1*, *i0*, *s1*, *s0*, and *d*, and we can name the entity *Mux4*, as shown in Figure 2.2(a). Figure 2.2(b) shows an entity declaration using those names. We grouped ports *i3*, *i2*, *i1*, *i0*, and ports *s1*, *s0*, to enhance readability.

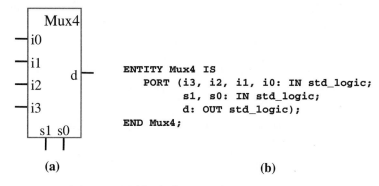

```
ENTITY Mux4 IS
    PORT (i3, i2, i1, i0: IN std_logic;
          s1, s0: IN std_logic;
          d: OUT std_logic);
END Mux4;
```

(a)   (b)

Figure 2.2 4x1 mux: (a) block diagram, (b) entity declaration.

ARCHITECTURES AND PROCESSES

The second part of a design entity's definition is an architecture body. While the first part, the entity declaration, defined the entity's *interface* to the outside world, an **architecture body** defines what is *inside* the entity. In other words, the architecture body describes the function of the entity, namely, how the entity's outputs are related to the entity's inputs. Notice in Figure 2.1 that the inputs and outputs of the *And2* entity and of the *Or2* entity are identical to one another; their architecture bodies will describe how those entities differ.

Figure 2.3 shows a complete entity definition, including both an entity declaration and an architecture body named *And2_beh* (note that other names could have been used), for an *And2* entity. Many ways exist to describe an architecture body. One way uses a process. A **process** describes behavior using a sequence of statements that are executed and then repeated. *A process thus describes an infinite loop.*

The process in Figure 2.3 begins with "*PROCESS(x, y)*", meaning the process only executes its statements if the value of *x* or of *y* changes, where "*(x, y)*" defines the process' sensitivity list. The **sensitivity list** of a process is a list of the signals to which the process is sensitive, meaning the process will only execute its statements whenever the value of any of the signals within the process' sensitivity list changes. The process shown contains a single statement, "*F <= x AND y;*", which computes the logical AND of *x* and *y*, and assigns the result to *F. AND* is a built-in operator in VHDL. "<=" is the symbol for assigning a value to a port (or any signal; more later). That symbol consists of two characters, "<" and

"=", intended to create the appearance of an arrow pointing to the left. Processes will be described in more detail later.

Figure 2.4 shows entity declarations and architecture bodies for *Or2* and *Inv* entities. The processes use the operators *OR* and *NOT*, both built-in operators in VHDL.

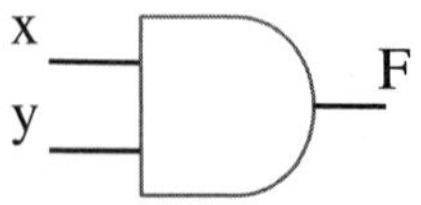

```
ENTITY And2 IS
    PORT (x: IN std_logic;
          y: IN std_logic;
          F: OUT std_logic);
END And2;

ARCHITECTURE And2_beh OF And2 IS
BEGIN

    PROCESS(x, y)
    BEGIN
        F <= x AND y;
    END PROCESS;

END And2_beh;
```

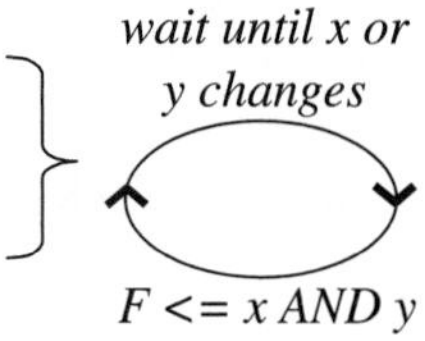

wait until x or y changes

$F <= x \, AND \, y$

Figure 2.3 Entity declaration and architecture body for a 2-input AND gate named *And2*.

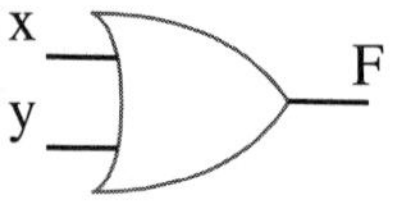

```
ENTITY Or2 IS
    PORT (x: IN std_logic;
          y: IN std_logic;
          F: OUT std_logic);
END Or2;

ARCHITECTURE Or2_beh OF Or2 IS
BEGIN

    PROCESS(x, y)
    BEGIN
        F <= x OR y;
    END PROCESS;

END Or2_beh;
```

(a)

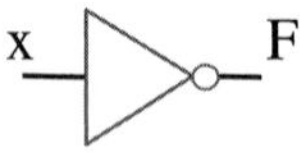

```
ENTITY Inv IS
    PORT (x: IN std_logic;
          F: OUT std_logic);
END Inv;

ARCHITECTURE Inv_beh OF Inv IS
BEGIN

    PROCESS(x)
    BEGIN
        F <= NOT x;
    END PROCESS;

END Inv_beh;
```

(b)

Figure 2.4 Entity declarations and architecture bodies for: (a) an OR gate, (b) a NOT gate.

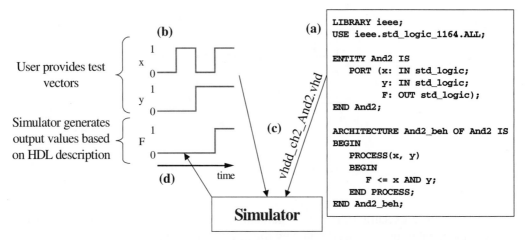

```
LIBRARY ieee;
USE ieee.std_logic_1164.ALL;

ENTITY And2 IS
    PORT (x: IN std_logic;
          y: IN std_logic;
          F: OUT std_logic);
END And2;

ARCHITECTURE And2_beh OF And2 IS
BEGIN
    PROCESS(x, y)
    BEGIN
        F <= x AND y;
    END PROCESS;
END And2_beh;
```

Figure 2.5 Simulating an entity: (a) User provides the entity definition and (b) the test vectors, (c) simulator reads entity definition and test vectors, and (d) simulator generates output values.

[SIMUL] SIMULATION AND TESTBENCHES—A FIRST LOOK

Given a newly-defined entity, one may wish to see how the entity behaves. In other words, for particular input values, what will be the entity's output values? *Simulation* is a procedure wherein a tool, known as a simulator, automatically generates output values for a given entity and a given sequence of input values.

Before applying simulation, a designer must define the sequence of input values that we wish to provide to the entity during the simulation. A designer will likely want to provide many different values on each input. For example, for a 2-input AND gate, we might provide input values *yx=00*, *yx=01*, *yx=10*, and *yx=11*, as shown in Figure 2.5(b). Each unique combination of input values is known as a ***test vector***. The figure shows those values graphically, using what are known as ***waveforms***. Some simulators allow users to describe test vectors by drawing waveforms using a graphical tool. The simulator then reads those test vectors and the entity definition file shown in Figure 2.5(c), and automatically generates output waveforms, as illustrated in Figure 2.5(d). Note that the entity definition file begins with *LIBRARY* and *USE* statements, which we have not yet defined; they are needed in order to use the *std_logic* type, and will be described later.

Simulators differ in how they allow users to create input waveforms. Rather than using a simulator's waveform creation capabilities, one can instead describe test vectors in an HDL itself, as illustrated in Figure 2.6. The first statement sets *yx=00*. The next statement, "*WAIT FOR 10 ns;*", tells the simulator to hold those values for 10 nanoseconds of simu-

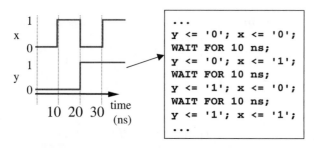

Figure 2.6 Creating test vectors in an HDL.

lated time, before executing the next statement, which sets *yx=01*. The resulting test vectors are identical to the vectors defined by the graphical waveforms.

A **testbench** is a setup for applying test vectors to test a design. Figure 2.7 shows the general setup of a testbench. The setup creates an entity called *Testbench* having no inputs or outputs. The setup instantiates a component representing the entity to be simulated, in this case named *CompToTest* and representing an *And2* entity. The setup uses a process that writes to signals *x_s* and *y_s,* which are connected to the inputs of *CompToTest*. The process will contain statements that set the signals with the desired test vectors, as was shown in Figure 2.6.

Figure 2.8 shows a complete VHDL testbench for an *And2* entity, following Figure 2.7's setup. The testbench is an entity named *Testbench* (though we could have used a different name). The entity has no inputs or outputs. The entity's architecture declares an *And2* component, declares several signals (*x_s, y_s,* and *F_s*), instantiates one instance of an *And2* component and names it *CompToTest*, and maps the signals to the component's ports. The next section will describe components, signals, instantiation, and port maps in more detail. Finally, the architecture defines a process that sets the *x_s* and *y_s* signals to the particular values at the desired times. Testbench format will be discussed further in Section 2.2.

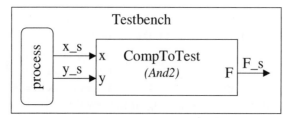

Figure 2.7 General setup of a testbench.

```
LIBRARY ieee;
USE ieee.std_logic_1164.ALL;

ENTITY Testbench IS
END Testbench;

ARCHITECTURE TBarch OF Testbench IS
    COMPONENT And2 IS
        PORT (x: IN std_logic;
              y: IN std_logic;
              F: OUT std_logic);
    END COMPONENT;

    SIGNAL x_s, y_s, F_s: std_logic;

BEGIN
    CompToTest: And2 PORT MAP (x_s, y_s, F_s);

    PROCESS
    BEGIN
        -- Test all possible input combinations
        y_s <= '0'; x_s <= '0';
        WAIT FOR 10 ns;
        y_s <= '0'; x_s <= '1';
        WAIT FOR 10 ns;
        y_s <= '1'; x_s <= '0';
        WAIT FOR 10 ns;
        y_s <= '1'; x_s <= '1';
        WAIT;
    END PROCESS;
END TBarch;
```

Figure 2.8 Testbench for *And2* entity.

WAIT statements

Unlike the process of Figure 2.3, the process in the testbench of Figure 2.8 has no sensitiv-ity list, meaning that the process should begin executing its statements right away rather than waiting for a change on some signal. The first two statements set y_s to 0 and x_s to 0. Note that two statements can appear on one line, but their meaning is the same as if they had appeared on two lines. The third statement is a wait statement. A *wait statement* in a process tells the simulator to suspend execution of the process. The statement can tell the simulator how long to wait before resuming execution, by using a *timeout clause*, such as "*WAIT FOR 10 ns;*". Thus, the process of Figure 2.8 effectively holds y_s and x_s at 00 for ten nanoseconds, before executing the next statement, which sets y_s and x_s to 01. The rest of the process behaves similarly, holding y_s and x_s at 01 for ten nanoseconds, then at 10 for ten nanoseconds, and finally holding them at 11. Those statements thus describe the

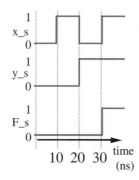

Figure 2.9 Waveforms generated by simulation for an *And2* entity.

waveforms for *y_s* and *x_s* shown in Figure 2.9. Note that all times described above correspond to simulated time, not real time.

The last statement of this process is *"WAIT;"*, which does not have a timeout clause. That statement suspends the process execution forever, or more specifically, until the simulator terminates simulation. In other words, this process executes only once, and does not repeat. That statement is necessary because a process is like an infinite loop, normally following execution of its last statement by execution of its first statement again; that final WAIT statement prevents such further execution.

One might save the testbench in a file, say *vhdd_ch2_And2TB.vhd*. Providing that file and the *vhdd_ch2_And.vhd* file to a simulator would then result in the simulator generating the waveforms shown in Figure 2.9. The waveforms show that the entity indeed behaves like a 2-input AND gate, outputting *1* only when both inputs are *1*s.

COMMENTS

Figure 2.8 contained the text "-- *Test all possible input combinations*". That text is known as a comment. A *comment* is text in HDL code intended only to be read by humans, and not to be read by a simulator or other tool. A comment begins with two hyphens: "--". All text on the remainder of the same line will be ignored by tools that read the HDL file. Comments enhance the readability of code, primarily by explaining to people the purpose of various parts of the code. In Figure 2.8, the comments make clear that the tests vectors are intended to test all possible combinations of the inputs, something that might otherwise take some time to discern by someone reading the code. Comments should assume the reader understands the language itself, and thus need not state the obvious, such as "-- *component instantiations*". A comment may follow a statement on the same line, such as:

```
      IF (L='1') THEN   -- Light detected
```

However, the opposite—a statement following a comment—is not true, because the statement would be considered part of the comment and would thus be ignored.

In addition to explanatory comments throughout code, it is customary to include comments at the top of a file and even before each entity, to describe the file's contents, the author, the authorship date, and other such information.

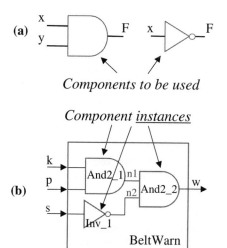

Figure 2.10 Components: (a) to be used, (b) instantiated.

2.2 COMBINATIONAL CIRCUIT STRUCTURE

A **circuit**, also known as **structure**, is a connection of components. Figure 2.10(b) provides an example of a circuit. A circuit represents a second way of describing the architecture of an entity, in contrast to a process as in the previous section.

COMPONENT INSTANTIATIONS

When used in a circuit, an entity—such as the AND, OR, or NOT entity defined in the previous section—is known as a **component**. Given the types of components to be used in a circuit, such as the 2-input AND component and the NOT component shown in Figure 2.10(a), **instantiating** a component means to bring into being a unique copy of the component, with each copy known as a component **instance**. The circuit in Figure 2.10(b) has two instances of a two-input AND gate component, and one instance of a NOT gate component. As an everyday example of instances, a car is built from several types of components, such as tires, engines, and windows. A car may have four tire instances, one engine instance, and six window instances.

Consider creating a new entity that turns on a warning light (by setting an output w to 1) if a car's key is in the car's ignition slot (indicated by an input k being 1), and a passenger is seated (indicated by an input p being 1), and the passenger's seat belt is not buckled (indicated by an input s being 0). One way to define such an entity is to use the circuit shown in Figure 2.10(b).

Creating a new entity in VHDL having a circuit architecture, like the circuit in Figure 2.10(b), involves several steps:

```
LIBRARY ieee;
USE ieee.std_logic_1164.ALL;

ENTITY BeltWarn IS
    PORT (k, p, s: IN std_logic;                    }  (a)
            w: OUT std_logic);
END BeltWarn;

ARCHITECTURE Circuit OF BeltWarn IS

    COMPONENT And2 IS
        PORT (x,y: IN std_logic;
                F: OUT std_logic);
    END COMPONENT;
                                                    }  (b)

    COMPONENT Inv IS
        PORT (x: IN std_logic;
                F: OUT std_logic);
    END COMPONENT;

    SIGNAL n1, n2: std_logic;                       }  (c)

BEGIN
    And2_1: And2 PORT MAP (k, p, n1);
    Inv_1:  Inv  PORT MAP (s, n2);                  }  (d)
    And2_2: And2 PORT MAP (n1, n2, w);
END Circuit;
```

Figure 2.11 Architecture defined as a circuit for the *BeltWarn* entity: (a) entity declaration, (b) component declarations, (c) signal declarations, (d) component instantiations.

1. Declare a new entity, as in Figure 2.11(a).

2. Declare the components to be used in the circuit, as in Figure 2.11(b). A *component declaration* defines the component's name and the component's input and output ports, which should be the same as in the component's original entity.

3. Declare signals for internal wires to be used to connect the components, as in Figure 2.11(c). To do this step, we should have drawn the desired circuit so that we know how many internal wires we'll need, and we should create unique names for each internal wire, as in Figure 2.10(b).

4. Instantiate components and create connections, as in Figure 2.11(d). To do this, we should have created unique names for each component instance in our drawn circuit, as in Figure 2.10(b).

The last step uses component instantiation statements. A *component instantiation* statement, shown in Figure 2.12, creates a single instance of a component in a circuit, and describes how that instance connects with circuit signals. Components must have been declared before they can be instantiated.

The first part of the component instantiation statement is a unique name for the component instance, and the second part indicates the type of component being instantiated. Fig-

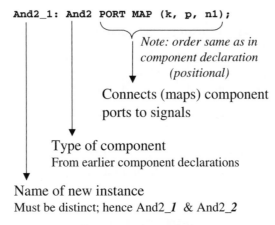

```
And2_1: And2 PORT MAP (k, p, n1);
```

Note: order same as in
component declaration
(positional)

Connects (maps) component
ports to signals

Type of component
From earlier component declarations

Name of new instance
Must be distinct; hence And2_*1* & And2_*2*

Figure 2.12 Component instantiation statement.

ure 2.11(d) instantiates three component instances: an instance named *And2_1* of type *And2*, an instance named *Inv_1* of type *Inv*, and an instance named *And2_2* of type *And2*. Using numbers at the end of the instance names (e.g., "*_1*" or "*_2*") is one way to create unique names. Note that any unique identifiers could have been used for the instance names, such as *Comp1*, *Comp2*, and *Comp3*.

SIGNALS AND PORT MAPS

The third part of a component instantiation statement, further illustrated in Figure 2.12, is the port map part. The ***port map*** part of a component instantiation statement connects the component instance's ports to the signals in the circuit.

A ***signal*** is an object that holds, or stores, a value at a particular time. A signal is similar to a variable in traditional programming languages, such as C, C++, or Java, in that both signals and variables store values, but signals differ from variables due to signal values being explicitly specified for particular simulated times. During simulation, a signal will hold its value for a particular simulated time. For example, Figure 2.9 shows a signal *y_s* that has a value of *0* from time 0 ns to time 20 ns, and a value of *1* from time 20 ns to time 40 ns. A signal may be explicitly declared using a ***signal declaration*** statement, as in Figure 2.11(c). Such signals are useful to represent internal wires of a circuit, as shown in Figure 2.10(b). All ports are also signals. Thus, there are six signals in Figure 2.11: The explicitly declared signals *n1* and *n2*, and the entity's ports *k*, *p*, *s*, and *w*. Signal declarations may appear within an architecture, but not within other constructs such as a process.

Each port map has a list of signals in parentheses. Each signal in the list connects to a port of the component, according to the order of ports in the component declaration, referred to as a ***positional*** port map. For example, component instance *And2_1* in Figure 2.11(d) is an *And2* component, which has ports *x*, *y*, and *F*. The component instantiation statement "*And2_1: And2 PORT MAP (k, p, n1);*" thus connects *(k, p, n1)* to *And2_1*'s ports *(x, y, F)*. In other words, the statement connects *k* to the *And2_1*'s *x* port, *p* to *And2_1*'s *y* port, and *n1* to *And2_1*'s *F* port.

Example 2.2: Creating a circuit using component instantiations

This example creates a VHDL entity for a 2x1 multiplexor, defining the mux's architecture using a circuit. Figure 2.13(a) shows a block diagram for a 2x1 mux.

We'll follow the four-step procedure defined earlier:

1. We create an entity declaration for a 2x1 mux with the proper inputs and outputs, shown in Figure 2.13(b).

2. We define the components to be used in the circuit, shown graphically in Figure 2.13(c), and using component declaration statements in Figure 2.13(d).

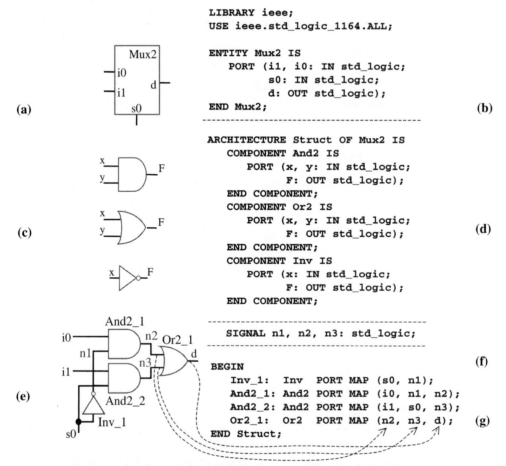

Figure 2.13 2x1 mux circuit example: (a) block diagram, (b) entity declaration, (c) components to be used, (d) component declarations, (e) desired circuit with components and internal wires labeled, (f) signal declarations for internal wires, (g) component instantiation statements.

3. We define the signals needed for internal wires, which we named *n1*, *n2*, and *n3*, as shown in Figure 2.13(f). Note that we should have sketched the circuit in Figure 2.13(e) in order to know how many internal wires will be needed.

4. Given the circuit in Figure 2.13(e), we instantiate components and create connections using component instantiation statements as in Figure 2.13(g).

■

[SIMUL] SIMULATING THE CIRCUIT

Simulating an entity whose architecture is defined as a circuit is no different than simulating an entity whose architecture is defined as a process. We simply create a testbench that instantiates the entity as a component, and that provides input values using a process, as was done in Section 2.1. Figure 2.14 shows the setup of a testbench for the *BeltWarn* entity

Figure 2.15 shows a VHDL testbench for the *BeltWarn* entity. The testbench has a similar format to the testbench shown in Figure 2.8. Note several features of the standard testbench format. First, note that the testbench uses a component instantiation statement. Second, note that the testbench declares signals *k_s*, *p_s*, *s_s*, and *w_s,* corresponding to the instantiated component's ports *k*, *p*, *s*, and *w*. Those signals are needed because the process that follows *cannot* directly access the component instance's ports, whereas the process *can* access the declared signals. We chose to append "*_s*" to the signal names to clearly distinguish those signals from the ports. Finally, note that an architecture can consist of both a component instantiation statement and a process statement. Each such statement is known as a **concurrent statement**. An architecture can have any number of concurrent statements, all of which behave as though they execute in parallel to jointly describe an entity's overall behavior.

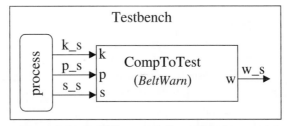

Figure 2.14 *BeltWarn* entity's testbench setup.

```
LIBRARY ieee;
USE ieee.std_logic_1164.ALL;

ENTITY Testbench IS
END Testbench;

ARCHITECTURE TBarch OF Testbench IS
    COMPONENT BeltWarn IS
        PORT (k, p, s: IN std_logic;
              w: OUT std_logic);
    END COMPONENT;

    SIGNAL k_s, p_s, s_s, w_s: std_logic;

BEGIN
    CompToTest: BeltWarn
        PORT MAP (k_s, p_s, s_s, w_s);

    PROCESS
    BEGIN
        k_s <= '0'; p_s <= '0'; s_s <= '0';
        WAIT FOR 10 ns;
        k_s <= '0'; p_s <= '1'; s_s <= '0';
        WAIT FOR 10 ns;
        k_s <= '1'; p_s <= '1'; s_s <= '0';
        WAIT FOR 10 ns;
        k_s <= '1'; p_s <= '1'; s_s <= '1';
        WAIT FOR 10 ns;
        WAIT;
    END PROCESS;
END TBarch;
```

Figure 2.15 Testbench for *BeltWarn* entity.

The testbench defines four test vectors, setting the *BeltWarn* component's inputs k, p, and s to *000*, *010*, *110*, and *111*, holding each test vector for 10 nanoseconds of simulated time. Figure 2.16 shows the waveforms resulting from simulating the testbench.

Because the component has three binary inputs, the number of possible test vectors is $2^3 = 8$. A complete testbench would generate all eight such vectors. Creating a complete testbench becomes increasingly difficult for components with more inputs, because the number of test vectors increases exponentially, requiring 2^n test vectors for a combinational circuit with n inputs. We will later discuss strategies to cope with the problem of too many test vectors.

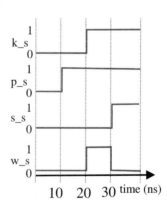

Figure 2.16 Waveforms generated by simulation of testbench for *BeltWarn*.

2.3 TOP-DOWN DESIGN—COMBINATIONAL BEHAVIOR TO STRUCTURE

Early in the design process, a designer may know the behavior of a system, but may not yet have designed the structure. For example, for the *BeltWarn* example, a designer may know that the desired behavior is $w = kps'$, but may not yet have designed the circuit shown in Figure 2.10(b). Designers therefore commonly follow a top-down design approach. In a ***top-down design approach***, illustrated in Figure 2.17, a designer first captures a system's behavior and simulates the system, and then creates the system's structure and simulates the system again. If the designer created the system structure correctly, then the behavior and structure simulations should yield identical waveforms. Following a top-down design process enables a designer to focus first on getting the behavior right, unfettered by the details of designing structure. The *BeltWarn* example is a small example — larger examples might have complex behavior that could be difficult to get right, making a top-down approach highly advantageous.

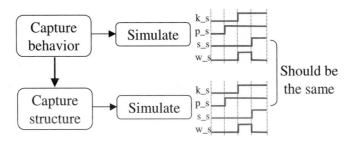

Figure 2.17 Top-down design process.

PROCESSES WITH SIGNAL ASSIGNMENT STATEMENTS

A common way to describe a system's behavior is to use a process. The simplest process contains a single signal assignment statement. A process describing the *BeltWarn* system's behavior appears in Figure 2.18. The process is sensitive to signals k, p, and s (recall that ports are signals), meaning the process executes whenever a value changes on one of those signals. The process contains a signal assignment that sets output port w to the appropriate value. The testbench for this entity would be the same testbench as appears in Figure 2.15, with no modifications. Simulating that testbench would result in the waveforms of Figure 2.16. Following a top-down design approach, a designer might then create the circuit

```
LIBRARY ieee;
USE ieee.std_logic_1164.ALL;

ENTITY BeltWarn IS
   PORT (k, p, s: IN std_logic;
           w: OUT std_logic);
END BeltWarn;

ARCHITECTURE Behav OF BeltWarn IS
BEGIN

   PROCESS (k, p, s)
   BEGIN
      w <= k AND p AND NOT(s);
   END PROCESS;

END Behav;
```

Figure 2.18 *BeltWarn* behavior described using a process with a single signal

shown in Figure 2.10(b), and simulate the system again using the same testbench, resulting in the same waveforms.

A *signal assignment statement* assigns a value to a signal. The left side of the assignment operator "<=" must be a signal. The right side may be an expression involving operators. Built-in logical operators include AND, OR, NOT, NAND, NOR, XOR, and XNOR. As an example, consider creating a process to compute $f = c'h + ch'$. The process would be defined sensitive to c and h as follows: "*PROCESS(c,h)*". The process could then contain the signal assignment statement: "*f <= (NOT(c) AND h) OR (c AND NOT(h));*". Alternatively, the process could instead contain the signal assignment statement: "*f <= c XOR h;*".

Note that a process may have more than one signal assignment statement. Figure 2.19 shows a process having two signal assignment statements.

```
LIBRARY ieee;
USE ieee.std_logic_1164.ALL;

ENTITY TwoOutputEx IS
   PORT (a, b, c: IN std_logic;
           F, G: OUT std_logic);
END TwoOutputEx;

ARCHITECTURE beh OF TwoOutputEx IS
BEGIN
   PROCESS(a, b, c)
   BEGIN
      F <= (a AND b) OR NOT(c);
      G <= (a AND b) OR (b AND c);
   END PROCESS;
END beh;
```

Figure 2.19 Two signal assignment statements in a process.

PROCESSES WITH IF STATEMENTS

In addition to having a signal assignment statement, a process may have other kinds of statements, such as an IF statement. An ***IF statement*** starts with "*IF (condition) THEN*". If the condition evaluates to true, then the statements following the *THEN* keyword are executed. For example, Figure 2.20 shows behavior for the *BeltWarn* example using a process having an *IF* statement. If the *IF* condition evaluates to true, the statement "*w <= '1';*" executes. If the *IF* condition instead evaluates to false, the statements following the *THEN* are skipped, and instead the statements following the *ELSE* keyword are executed, namely "*w <= '0';*". The *ELSE* part of an *IF* statement is optional. An *IF* statement always ends with "*END IF;*", regardless of whether or not an *ELSE* part exists.

```
LIBRARY ieee;
USE ieee.std_logic_1164.ALL;

ENTITY BeltWarn IS
    PORT (k, p, s: IN std_logic;
            w: OUT std_logic);
END BeltWarn;

ARCHITECTURE Behav OF BeltWarn IS
BEGIN

    PROCESS (k, p, s)
    BEGIN
        IF ((k AND p AND NOT(s)) = '1') THEN
            w <= '1';
        ELSE
            w <= '0';
        END IF;
    END PROCESS;

END Behav;
```

Figure 2.20 *BeltWarn* behavior described using a process having an IF statement.

Note that the condition shown is not just "*(k AND p AND NOT(s))*". That condition would evaluate to either *'0'* or *'1'* rather than to a Boolean value of false or true. Instead, the condition includes a comparison with *'1'* (" = *'1'*") so that the condition evaluates to false or true. Alternatively, the condition "*(k='1' AND p='1' AND s='0')*" could be used, because each comparison results in a false or true, resulting in the condition evaluating to false or true. Note that logical operators can be used on Boolean values but cannot be combined with logic values of *'0'* or *'1'* in the same expression.

An *IF* statement can have one or more *ELSIF* parts to handle more possible conditions. The first part whose condition evaluates to true will have its statements executed, and the remaining parts will be skipped. Figure 2.21 shows a process having an *IF* statement with two *ELSIF* parts and an *ELSE* part, describing the behavior of a 4x1 multiplexor. The figure shows which particular statements would be executed if the process were executed with

```
LIBRARY ieee;
USE ieee.std_logic_1164.ALL;

ENTITY Mux4 IS
   PORT (i3, i2, i1, i0: IN std_logic;
         s1, s0: IN std_logic;
         d: OUT std_logic);
END Mux4;

ARCHITECTURE Beh OF Mux4 IS
BEGIN

   PROCESS(i3, i2, i1, i0, s1, s0)
   BEGIN
     IF (s1='0' AND s0='0') THEN
        d <= i0;
     ELSIF (s1='0' AND s0='1') THEN
        d <= i1;
     ELSIF (s1='1' AND s0='0') THEN
        d <= i2;
     ELSE
        d <= i3;
     END IF;
   END PROCESS;

END Beh;
```

Figure 2.21 4x1 mux described using a process having an IF statement with ELSIF and ELSE parts.

s1s0=01. The *IF*'s condition evaluates to false, so its statement "*d <= i0;*" would be skipped. The first *ELSIF*'s condition evaluates to true, so its statement "*d <= i1;*" would execute, and the remaining parts of the *IF* statement would be skipped. The last part need not be *ELSE*, but if an *ELSE* part exists, it must be the last part.

Example 2.3: 2x4 decoder

This example describes a 2x4 decoder's behavior using a process having an *IF* statement. The entity declaration appears in Figure 2.22, having inputs *i1* and *i0*. The architecture has

```
LIBRARY ieee;
USE ieee.std_logic_1164.ALL;

ENTITY Dcd2x4 IS
   PORT (i1, i0: IN std_logic;
         d3, d2, d1, d0: OUT std_logic);
END Dcd2x4;

ARCHITECTURE Beh OF Dcd2x4 IS
BEGIN
   PROCESS(i1, i0)
   BEGIN
      IF (i1='0' AND i0='0') THEN
         d3 <= '0'; d2 <= '0';
         d1 <= '0'; d0 <= '1';
      ELSIF (i1='0' AND i0='1') THEN
         d3 <= '0'; d2 <= '0';
         d1 <= '1'; d0 <= '0';
      ELSIF (i1='1' AND i0='0') THEN
         d3 <= '0'; d2 <= '1';
         d1 <= '0'; d0 <= '0';
      ELSIF (i1='1' AND i0='1') THEN
         d3 <= '1'; d2 <= '0';
         d1 <= '0'; d0 <= '0';
      END IF;
   END PROCESS;
END Beh;
```

Figure 2.22 2x4 decoder described using a process having an IF statement.

a process that is sensitive to the inputs *i1* and *i0*. The process contains a single *IF* statement whose four parts detect each of the four possible conditions of *i1i0 = 00, 01, 10,* or *11*.

Note that two (or more) signal assignment statements (or other types of statements) may appear on a single line. New lines and extra spaces have no impact other than enhancing readability of the code.

Note that the *IF* statement has no *ELSE* part in this example. Instead, the last part is an *ELSIF* part detecting the condition *i1i0=11*. We could replace this part simply by an *ELSE* part, which has no condition, because the only way the *ELSE* part could be reached would be if *i1i0=11*. However, using *ELSIF* and showing the condition explicitly, as in the figure, may result in code that is more readable.

_____ ∎

MULTIPLE ARCHITECTURES FOR ONE ENTITY

A top-down design process involves capturing two architectures for the same entity—first an architecture described behaviorally, and then an architecture described structurally. Fortunately, the first architecture need not be deleted in order to capture the second architecture. Instead, a single entity may have two (or more) architectures describing the entity's

```
LIBRARY ieee;
USE ieee.std_logic_1164.ALL;

ENTITY BeltWarn IS
    PORT (k, p, s: IN std_logic;
            w: OUT std_logic);
END BeltWarn;
---------------------------------------------------
ARCHITECTURE Behav OF BeltWarn IS
BEGIN
    PROCESS (k, p, s)
    BEGIN
       w <= k AND p AND NOT(s);
    END PROCESS;
END Behav;
---------------------------------------------------
ARCHITECTURE Circuit OF BeltWarn IS
    COMPONENT And2 IS
        PORT (x,y: IN std_logic;
                F: OUT std_logic);
    END COMPONENT;
    COMPONENT Inv IS
        PORT (x: IN std_logic;
                F: OUT std_logic);
    END COMPONENT;
    SIGNAL n1, n2: std_logic;
BEGIN
    And2_1: And2 PORT MAP (k, p, n1);
    Inv_1:  Inv  PORT MAP (s, n2);
    And2_2: And2 PORT MAP (n1, n2, w);
END Circuit;
```

Figure 2.23 *BeltWarn* entity with two architectures, one behavioral, one structural.

internal design. For example, Figure 2.23 shows a *BeltWarn* entity with two architectures, one behavioral, the other structural. A designer might first capture the entity declaration and behavioral architecture (called *Behav* in the figure) in a single file, and simulate using the testbench in Figure 2.15. The designer might then add the structural architecture (called *Circuit* in the figure) simply by adding to the bottom of the same file.

During simulation, only one architecture can be used. While VHDL does have a way for specifying to a simulator which architecture to use (via **configuration statements**), many simulators provide simple mechanisms for selecting which architecture to use, and designers commonly use those mechanisms.

COMMON PITFALLS

Certain mistakes are made frequently. Such mistakes are known as **common pitfalls**. We describe a few common pitfalls that occur when describing combinational behavior using a process. Recall that for combinational behavior, the output value is purely a function of the

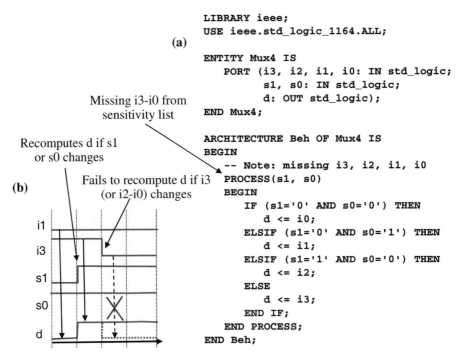

```
                                    LIBRARY ieee;
                                    USE ieee.std_logic_1164.ALL;
                       (a)
                                    ENTITY Mux4 IS
                                        PORT (i3, i2, i1, i0: IN std_logic;
                                              s1, s0: IN std_logic;
         Missing i3-i0 from                   d: OUT std_logic);
         sensitivity list           END Mux4;

                                    ARCHITECTURE Beh OF Mux4 IS
   Recomputes d if s1               BEGIN
   or s0 changes                        -- Note: missing i3, i2, i1, i0
                                        PROCESS(s1, s0)
(b)     Fails to recompute d if i3      BEGIN
        (or i2-i0) changes                 IF (s1='0' AND s0='0') THEN
                                              d <= i0;
 i1                                        ELSIF (s1='0' AND s0='1') THEN
                                              d <= i1;
 i3                                        ELSIF (s1='1' AND s0='0') THEN
                                              d <= i2;
 s1                                        ELSE
                                              d <= i3;
 s0                                        END IF;
                                        END PROCESS;
 d                                  END Beh;
```

Figure 2.24 Incorrect description of a 4x1 mux: (a) sensitivity list with missing inputs, (b) undesired behavior that appears during simulation.

present input values, whereas for sequential behavior, the output value is a function of present and past input values, i.e., sequential behavior has memory.

Missing inputs from sensitivity list

When using a process to describe combinational behavior, one common pitfall is to not include all the entity's inputs in the process sensitivity list. Figure 2.24(a) provides an example of this mistake in a process that was intended to describe a 4x1 mux. The process sensitivity list is missing inputs $i3$, $i2$, $i1$, and $i0$. That omission results in an entity whose behavior does not correspond to a 4x1 mux. Figure 2.24(b) illustrates the incorrect behavior. Suppose initially that $s1s0=01$, so $d=i1$, and $i1$ happens to be '0'. If $s1$ or $s0$ changes, the process will execute, and recompute the correct value of the output d. In the figure, when $s1$ changes to '1', the process executes and sets $d=i3$, and $i3$ happens to be '1'. However, if $i3$, $i2$, $i1$, or $i0$ changes, the process will not execute. In the figure, $i3$ changes from '1' to '0', but the entity continues to output the old value of '1', because the process did not execute when $i3$ changed. Instead, the process should have again executed, and set $d=i3$, meaning '0'. Hence, the behavior has some form of memory, and is therefore sequential.

Note that this mistake is not a VHDL error. The code is legal VHDL. The code just does not describe a 4x1 mux.

(a)

```
LIBRARY ieee;
USE ieee.std_logic_1164.ALL;

ENTITY Dcd2x4 IS
    PORT (i1, i0: IN std_logic;
          d3, d2, d1, d0: OUT std_logic);
END Dcd2x4;

ARCHITECTURE Beh OF Dcd2x4 IS
BEGIN
    PROCESS(i1, i0)
    BEGIN
        IF (i1='0' AND i0='0') THEN
            d3 <= '0'; d2 <= '0';
            d1 <= '0'; d0 <= '1';
        ELSIF (i1='0' AND i0='1') THEN
            d3 <= '0'; d2 <= '0';
            d1 <= '1'; d0 <= '0';
        ELSIF (i1='1' AND i0='0') THEN
            d3 <= '0'; d2 <= '1';
            d1 <= '0'; d0 <= '0';
        ELSIF (i1='1' AND i0='1') THEN
            d3 <= '1';
        END IF;
        -- Note: missing assignments
        -- to all outputs in last ELSIF
    END PROCESS;
END Beh;
```

(b)

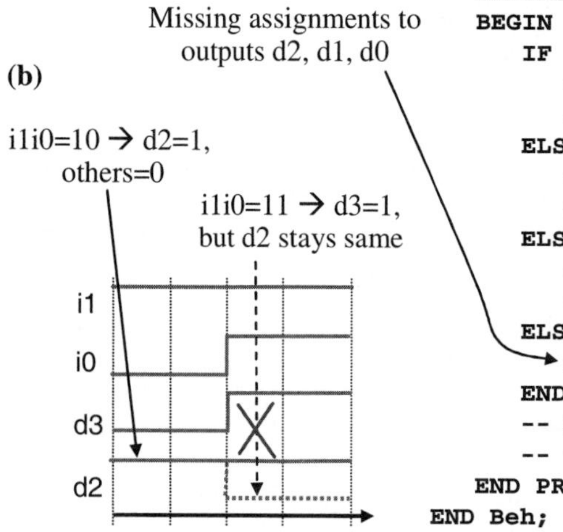

Missing assignments to outputs d2, d1, d0

$i1i0=10 \rightarrow d2=1$, others=0

$i1i0=11 \rightarrow d3=1$, but d2 stays same

i1

i0

d3

d2

Figure 2.25 Incorrect 2x4 decoder description: (a) some outputs not assigned on every pass, (b) incorrect behavior that appears during simulation.

Outputs not assigned on every pass

When using a process to describe combinational behavior, another common pitfall is to fail to assign every output on every possible pass through a process. Figure 2.25(a) provides an example of that mistake in a process that was intended to describe a 2x4 decoder. The last *ELSIF* part is missing assignments to *d2*, *d1*, and *d0*.

The omission results in a process whose behavior does not correspond to a 2x4 decoder. Figure 2.25(b) illustrates the incorrect behavior. Suppose initially that *i1i0=10*, and therefore that the output *d2* is '1' and all other outputs equal '0'. Suppose then that *i1i0* changes to "11" as shown. The process will execute, and the last *ELSIF* part will execute. However, that last *ELSIF* only has the statement "*d3 <= '1';*". Thus, *d3* will be updated to '1' as shown in Figure 2.25(b), but *d2* will also remain at '1' because it won't be explicitly set to '0' in that last *ELSIF* part. Hence, the circuit has some form of memory, and is therefore sequential.

Note that this mistake is not a VHDL error. The code is legal VHDL. The code just does not describe a 2x4 decoder.

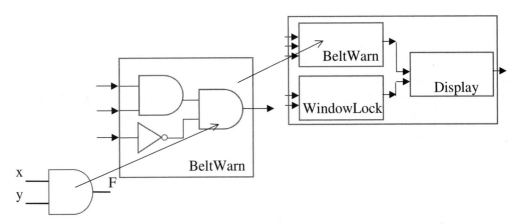

Figure 2.26 Hierarchy is a powerful mechanism for managing complexity.

The same pitfall occurs when not all input combinations are included in an *IF* statement. For example, a designer might forget to include the last *ELSIF* part entirely, thus not including the input combination *i1i0=11* in the *IF* statement. If *i1* or *i0* changes such that *i1i0=11*, the process would execute, but would reach the end of the process without executing any signal assignment statements. Thus, the output would remember the previous value, and hence the process would not describe a 2x4 decoder. This pitfall results in what is commonly referred to as an ***inferred latch***, because the process describes a circuit that must include a latch or some other form of memory (more on inferred latches later).

2.4 HIERARCHICAL CIRCUITS

After creating an entity (behaviorally or structurally), we may want to use that entity as a component in another design. We did this earlier when we created an *And2* entity, and then used that *And2* entity as a component in a circuit describing a *BeltWarn* entity, as shown in Figure 2.26. Likewise, we could use the *BeltWarn* entity as a component in another entity, as shown in the figure.

Hierarchy is the notion that an entity may be broken down into components, where each component itself may be broken down into components, and so on. Hierarchy is a powerful mechanism for managing complexity, since the designer of an entity need only think of a smaller number of components one level down, rather than having to think of a larger numbers of components at the bottom level.

USING ENTITIES AS COMPONENTS

VHDL directly supports hierarchy by allowing an entity to be used as a component in another entity. We will demonstrate such hierarchy using an example.

Example 2.4: 4-bit 2x1 mux

Consider the design of a 4-bit 2x1 mux. We begin by first designing a 2x1 mux entity as a circuit built from gate-level components, as was done in Figure 2.13. Next, we design a 4-bit 2x1 mux as a circuit built from 2x1 mux components, as shown in Figure 2.27. The 4-bit 2x1 mux could then be used as a component in some other design, and so on.

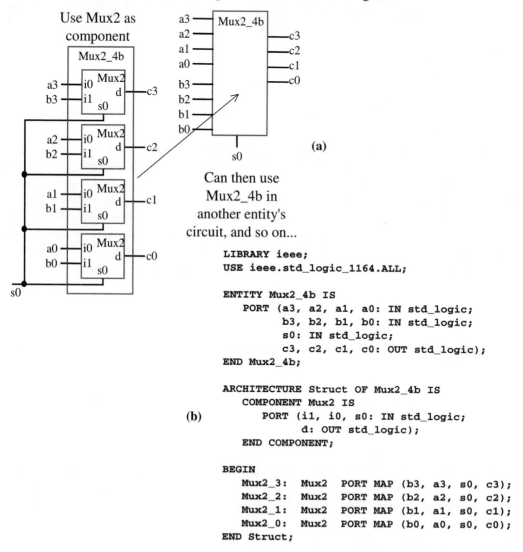

Can then use Mux2_4b in another entity's circuit, and so on...

```
LIBRARY ieee;
USE ieee.std_logic_1164.ALL;

ENTITY Mux2_4b IS
    PORT (a3, a2, a1, a0: IN std_logic;
          b3, b2, b1, b0: IN std_logic;
          s0: IN std_logic;
          c3, c2, c1, c0: OUT std_logic);
END Mux2_4b;

ARCHITECTURE Struct OF Mux2_4b IS
    COMPONENT Mux2 IS
        PORT (i1, i0, s0: IN std_logic;
              d: OUT std_logic);
    END COMPONENT;

BEGIN
    Mux2_3:  Mux2  PORT MAP (b3, a3, s0, c3);
    Mux2_2:  Mux2  PORT MAP (b2, a2, s0, c2);
    Mux2_1:  Mux2  PORT MAP (b1, a1, s0, c1);
    Mux2_0:  Mux2  PORT MAP (b0, a0, s0, c0);
END Struct;
```

(b)

Figure 2.27 Using hierarchy: (a) to build a 4-bit 2x1 mux from 2x1 muxes, (b) VHDL description.

CHAPTER 3

Sequential Logic Design

3.1 REGISTER BEHAVIOR

Sequential circuits store bits. A basic storage component is a register. A basic N-bit register can store N bits. Figure 3.1 illustrates a 4-bit register. That register has a clock input, a reset input (*rst*), four data inputs (*I3*, *I2*, *I1*, *I0*), and four data outputs (*Q3*, *Q2*, *Q1*, *Q0*). The register shown is loaded with its data inputs on every clock cycle. One approach to describing a 4-bit register is structurally, using 4 D flip-flops. However, another approach to describing a 4-bit register is behaviorally, an approach we now introduce.

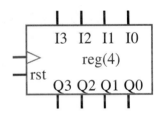

Figure 3.1 4-bit register.

SIGNALS AS STORAGE

Figure 3.2 shows a behavioral description of a 4-bit register. Briefly, the description consists of a single process that stores a new value into the 4-bit signal *Q* on every rising clock edge. If the reset input was '*1*' during that clock edge, the register stores "*0000*". Otherwise, the register stores into *Q* whatever values are on the 4-bit input *I*. We now explain various aspects of the register's description in more detail.

The entity declaration could have declared four 1-bit ports for the four data inputs *I3*, *I2*, *I1*, *I0*, as shown in Figure 3.3(a). Instead, the entity declaration declares one 4-bit port, *I*, by declaring *I* to be of type *std_logic_vector(3 DOWNTO 0)*, as in Figure 3.3(b). A **std_logic_vector** type defines a collection of bits, and is more convenient than defining each bit separately. The *std_logic_vector* declaration must specify the numbering and order of the bits within the vector, defined here as *3 DOWNTO 0*. Thus, the *3 DOWNTO 0* part

```
LIBRARY ieee;
USE ieee.std_logic_1164.ALL;

ENTITY Reg4 IS
    PORT (I: IN std_logic_vector(3 DOWNTO 0);
            Q: OUT std_logic_vector(3 DOWNTO 0);
            Clk, Rst: IN std_logic );
END Reg4;

ARCHITECTURE Beh OF Reg4 IS
BEGIN
    PROCESS (Clk)
    BEGIN
        IF (Clk = '1' AND Clk'EVENT) THEN
            IF (Rst = '1') THEN
                Q <= "0000";
            ELSE
                Q <= I;
            END IF;
        END IF;
    END PROCESS;
END Beh;
```

Figure 3.2 4-bit register description.

also defines how many bits exist. In this example, the bits are numbered from *3 DOWNTO 0*, meaning 3, 2, 1, 0, and thus there are four bits, as illustrated in Figure 3.3(b). We could have numbered the bits *0 TO 3,* or even *1 TO 4,* but convention usually puts the highest-order bit on the left and numbering typically begins at 0. Figure 3.2 declares the data outputs similarly to the data inputs, using one 4-bit port *Q* of type *std_logic_vector.*

To access an individual bit of a logic vector, we specify the bit position in parentheses, e.g., *Q(2) <= I(1)* would assign input bit 1 to output bit 2. The benefit of using a logic vector becomes evident when assigning multiple bits. For example, note in the description that, at one point, *Q* gets assigned to *I* using the statement "*Q <= I;*". That single statement actually represents four assignments: *Q(3) <= I(3)*, *Q(2) <= I(2)*, *Q(1) <= I(1)*, and *Q(0) <= I(0)*. As another example, note in the description that all four bits of *Q* are set to *0s* with one statement: "*Q(3) <= "0000";*". "*0000*" is the way to represent a four-bit *std_logic_vector*

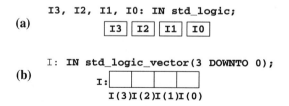

Figure 3.3. Two ways of declaring a 4-bit input: (a) as four bits, (b) as a 4-bit vector.

consisting of all *0*s. Similarly, *"0101"* would specify a four-bit *std_logic_vector* corresponding to the binary value *0101*, or decimal value of 5.

The register's architecture has a single process sensitive only to the clock input. Unlike a combinational circuit, a register's data outputs are not affected directly by changes on the register's data inputs; instead, only on a rising clock edge does the register load the data inputs. Thus, the process is only sensitive to the clock input *Clk*. When the process executes, meaning there was a change on the clock input, the first statement of the process compares *Clk* to '*1*' to determine if the change was a rising clock edge, as opposed to a falling clock edge. (That statement also checks that the clock signal actually changed, using *Clk'event*. That check is redundant in this example because the process is sensitive to *Clk* only, but good coding practice includes that check to make clear that the statement is detecting a rising clock edge). If the clock change was not a rising edge, then the process reaches the end, and waits for the next change on *Clk* due to the process' sensitivity list. If the clock change was in fact a rising edge, the process checks if the reset input *Rst* is '*1*'. If so, the register should be reset to *0*s, and the process does so with the statement "*Q <= "0000";*". If *Rst* was not '*1*', then the register should load the data inputs, which the process does using the statement "*Q <= I;*".

Notice that the register's contents will only be reset to all *0*s upon a rising clock edge when the *Rst* input is '*1*'. Thus, resetting the contents of the register to all *0*s will be synchronized with a rising clock edge. A reset synchronized with the clock edge is called a **synchronous reset**. An alternative reset implementation is an asynchronous reset, which will be described later in this chapter.

The register's storage is achieved by writing to port *Q*. Because a port is a signal and a signal implements storage, then writing to a port implements storage. *Q* will maintain its previously-written value until the next write to *Q*, thus achieving the desired storage of the register.

[SIMUL] TESTBENCHES WITH CLOCK SIGNALS

A testbench for a register component, illustrated in Figure 3.4, has a no-port entity declaration (not shown), a component declaration for the register (not shown), signal declarations, and a component instantiation similar to those of previously introduced testbenches. However, the register's testbench has two processes, rather than just one process as in previous testbenches.

The first process, named *ClkProcess*, generates values for the clock, with the clock having a 20 ns period. The process sets the clock to '*0*' for 10 ns, and then sets the clock to '*1*' for 10 ns. The process then immediately repeats itself, meaning the process sets the clock to '*0*' again for 10 ns, then to '*1*' again for 10 ns, and so on.

The second process, *VectorProcess*, serves the purpose seen in previous testbenches, namely of generating a component's input vectors.

```
      ...
         SIGNAL I_s, Q_s: std_logic_vector(3 DOWNTO 0);
         SIGNAL Clk_s: std_logic;

   BEGIN
         CompToTest: Reg4 PORT MAP (I_s, Q_s, Clk_s, Rst_s);

         ClkProcess: PROCESS
         BEGIN
            Clk_s <= '0';
            WAIT FOR 10 NS;
            Clk_s <= '1';
            WAIT FOR 10 NS;
         END PROCESS ClkProcess; -- Note: Process repeats

         VectorProcess: PROCESS
         BEGIN
            Rst_s <= '1';
            I_s <= "0000";
            WAIT UNTIL Clk_s='1' AND Clk_s'EVENT;
            WAIT FOR 5 NS;
            Rst_s <= '0';
            I_s <= "0000";
            WAIT UNTIL Clk_s='1' AND Clk_s'EVENT;
            WAIT FOR 5 NS;
            I_s <= "1010";
            WAIT UNTIL Clk_s='1' AND Clk_s'EVENT;
            WAIT FOR 5 NS;
            I_s <= "1111";
            WAIT;
         END PROCESS VectorProcess;
   END TBarch;
```

Figure 3.4 Register testbench.

In this example, notice that a process may have a name. Such names help clarify the purpose of the process. We specify the process name by including the name followed by a semicolon before the *PROCESS* keyword. For example, "*ClkProcess: PROCESS*" specifies the name of the process that generates the values for the clock signal in our testbench. Whenever a process name is specified, good practice dictates that we also include the name when ending the process. For the *ClkProcess*, this is accomplished with the "*END PRO-CESS ClkProcess;*" statement. Notice that the end process statement does not have a semi-colon between *END PROCESS* and the process name.

Notice also in this example that two processes may access the same signal. The clock signal *Clk_s* is accessed by the process *ClkProcess* and also by the process *VectorProcess*. However, only one process should write to a shared signal. (Actually, multiple processes could write to a signal in certain situations; this subject will be discussed in Section 4.5). *ClkProcess* writes the signal *Clk_s*, while *VectorProcess* reads the signal. Multiple pro-cesses may read a shared signal.

VectorProcess begins by resetting the register using "*Rst_s <= '1';*" Note that the process also sets *I_s* to "*0000*", even though such setting of *I_s* is really not necessary because the register internally sets itself to "*0000*" upon a reset. However, good practice dictates setting all of a component's inputs to some defined value at the beginning of a vector process, even if those values are not used. Such setting prevents the potential problem of forgetting to set a particular input value later in the vector process, which could lead to incorrect simulation results or unexpected behavior.

VectorProcess consists of four test vectors. The first vector resets the register, as discussed above. The second vector loads the register with "*0000*". The third vector loads "*1010*", and the fourth vector loads "*1111*". The first three vectors are followed by a *WAIT* statement, "*WAIT UNTIL Clk_s='1' AND Clk_s'EVENT;*" which waits for the next rising edge of the clock input. Only on that rising clock edge should the register be updated with the vector's values.

The *WAIT* statement represents another form of *WAIT* statement, "*WAIT UNTIL condition;*", which waits until the condition changes to true before moving on to the next statement. Note that we said "changes" to true — if the condition is initially true, the wait until statement waits for the condition to turn false, and then to turn true again. The condition obviously should contain at least one signal, whose value can change and thus which can cause the condition to change.

Before setting the register's inputs with the next vectors, the process waits for 5 ns. That extra wait seeks to make the simulation waveforms easier to read, by having the newly-loaded values appear separately from the next vectors, which appear 5 ns later.

Figure 3.5 shows waveforms that would be generated by the testbench of Figure 3.4. *Clk_s* alternates between '*1*' and '*0*' every 10 ns. *Rst_s* is initially '*1*'. Thus, when the first rising clock edge appears at time 10 ns, the register's output *Q* (connected in the testbench to the signal *Q_s*, which appears in the waveforms) resets to "*0000*". Note that before time 10 ns, *Q*'s value was undefined, indicated in the waveform as "*????*", because no value had yet been written to *Q*. Depending on your simulator, you may instead see a value of "*UUUU*" indicating *Q*'s value is undefined.

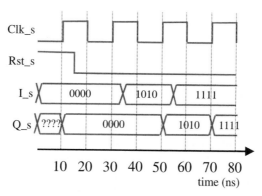

Figure 3.5 Register testbench waveforms.

Rst_s becomes '*0*' 5 ns later, at time 15 ns. *I* (connected to signal *I_s*, which appears in the waveform) is also set to "*0000*" at that time, but since *I* was earlier set to "*0000*", no change appears in *I*'s waveform. When the next rising clock edge appears, at time 30 ns, the register's output *Q* takes on the value on input *I*, which is "*0000*". *I* changes to "1010" 5 ns later. When the next rising clock edge appears, at time 50 ns, *Q* becomes "*1010*". The waveforms show that the register correctly loads its input *I* to its output *Q* only on rising clock edges.

[SIMUL] COMMON PITFALLS

Some common pitfalls exist when creating testbenches, which we now describe.

Omitting the final wait statement or not having any wait statements

A common pitfall is the omission of the final "*WAIT;*" statement at the end of the vector process in a testbench, as shown in Figure 3.6. Such omission causes the process to repeat, because when a process without a sensitivity list finishes executing its last statement, the process automatically executes its first statement again. Such repeated execution is typically not what was intended by the person who wrote the vector process. The final "*WAIT;*" statement tells the simulator that this process should no longer be executed, and thus the process will only execute once.

```
VectorProcess: PROCESS
BEGIN
    Rst_s <= '1';
    I_s <= "0000";
    WAIT UNTIL Clk_s='1' AND Clk_s'EVENT;
    WAIT FOR 5 NS;
    I_s <= "1111";
    WAIT;
END PROCESS VectorProcess;
```

Figure 3.6 Pitfall: Omitting the final WAIT.

Another common pitfall is to not include any wait statement at all in a process, nor to include a sensitivity list (which has the same effect as a particular form of wait statement), as illustrated in Figure 3.7. The failure to include at least one wait statement causes an infinite loop in a simulator. Although processes model concurrently-executing hardware modules, a simulator executes each process one at a time, executing each process up to the process' next wait statement before moving on to execute the next process. When the simulator has executed every process (that needs to be executed) once, the simulator updates the simulator's generated waveforms, and re-executes processes again. If a process has no wait statement (nor sensitivity list), then the simulator can never move on to the next process or update the simulator's waveforms. Instead, the simulator gets stuck in an infinite loop that repeatedly executes the statements of that process lacking any wait statement.

```
VectorProcess: PROCESS
BEGIN
    Rst_s <= '1';
    I_s <= "0000";
END PROCESS VectorProcess;
```

Figure 3.7   Pitfall: Not including any WAIT statement nor sensitivity list.

This pitfall is commonly encountered not just in testbench processes, but in other processes, too. For example, a common mistake is to forget to include a sensitivity list in a process that is supposed to describe combinational logic. When a process exists with no wait statement or sensitivity list, then running simulation results in the simulator not generating any waveforms. Instead, the simulator appears to just "hang" and do nothing, as shown in Figure 3.8. In fact, the simulator is doing plenty of work, but that work consists of repeatedly executing the process lacking a wait statement.

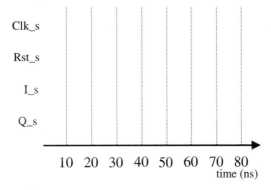

Figure 3.8   Pitfall: not including any WAIT or sensitivity list results in the simulator not generating any waveforms, instead appearing to just "hang."

To avoid the above pitfalls, some experienced designers write in the final "*WAIT;*" statement to the end of a testbench process immediately when they first start writing the process, before writing even the first test vectors.

Not initializing all input ports

A common pitfall is to forget to explicitly assign a value to every input port of a component being tested, as shown in Figure 3.9. A simulator will usually show such an un-initialized signal value by placing a "*?*" or "*U*" in the signal's waveform. While an undefined component input usually results in an undefined component output value, which is easy to detect by a designer, an undefined component input could result in a valid component output, depending on how the component's architecture was written. In that case, the valid output may not be what the designer expects, and tracing the problem back to an un-initialized

```
VectorProcess: PROCESS
BEGIN
    Rst_s <= '1';
    I_s <= "0000";
    WAIT UNTIL Clk_s='1' AND Clk_s'EVENT;
    WAIT FOR 5 NS;
    I_s <= "1111";
    WAIT;
END PROCESS VectorProcess;
```

Figure 3.9 Pitfall: Not initializing all input ports.

input can be difficult, especially when there are many input signals or when the undefined signal's waveform was not selected to be shown in the simulation output.

An even worse problem occurs if the simulator assigns a default value to every signal. Simulators are not supposed to do that, but not all simulators are perfectly compliant. The problem is that a testbench and design may simulate correctly under one simulator, but when that same testbench and design are run (perhaps years later) on another simulator that does not assign a default value, they may fail to simulate properly.

Therefore, when creating a testbench process, some experienced designers will immediately write statements that initialize all of a component's inputs, setting those inputs to *0*s, *1*s, or whatever is appropriate, before beginning to write the process' test vectors.

3.2 FINITE-STATE MACHINES (FSMS)—SEQUENTIAL BEHAVIOR

Finite-state machines (FSMs) are a standard way to describe the desired behavior of sequential circuits. Figure 3.10(a) shows an FSM having four states. One approach to modeling FSMs uses two processes, an approach we now describe.

ARCHITECTURES WITH USER-DEFINED TYPES, MULTIPLE PROCESSES, AND SHARED SIGNALS

Because FSMs eventually get implemented as a state register and combinational logic, as shown in Figure 3.10(b), a common approach for describing an FSM uses a two-process approach, illustrated in Figure 3.11. One process describes a state register for the FSM, and the other process describes the combinational function that computes the next state and the outputs based on the current state and inputs.

The description's architecture first declares a new type named *Statetype*. A **type** declaration defines a new name that represents a set of possible values. *Statetype* can represent four possible values: *S_Off*, *S_On1*, *S_On2*, and *S_On3*, values that we made up to correspond to the four states of the FSM. This type declaration is called an **enumeration type** because all possible values of the newly created type were enumerated within the declara-

Inputs: b; Outputs: x

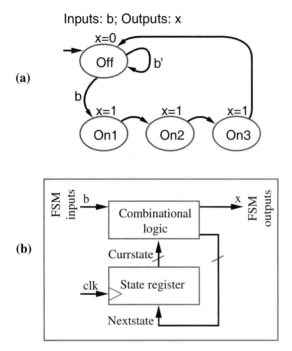

(a)

(b)

Figure 3.10 FSMs: (a) an FSM, (b) the sequential circuit implementation model.

tion. The description then declares two signals, *Currstate* and *Nextstate*, both of type *State-type*. Each signal can thus only take on values from the set of four values for *Statetype*.

The convention of using state names that begin with "*S_*" helps to make clear that those identifiers represent states. The convention also helps avoid conflicts with keywords — for example, *ON* is a VHDL reserved word, while *S_On* is not.

The two signals are shared by the two processes. According to Figure 3.10(b), the *CombLogic* process should be sensitive to *Currstate* and *b*, as shown in Figure 3.11, and will set values for *Nextstate* and *x*. The *StateReg* process models a register, and is thus sensitive only to the clock input *Clk*. The process will set a value for *Currstate*.

The *CombLogic* process can be described using the case statement shown in Figure 3.12. A **case statement** selects for execution one sequence among several possible sequences of statements, based on the value of an expression. In the figure, the expression is simply *Currstate*. The possible values of *Currstate* are *S_Off*, *S_On1*, *S_On2*, and *S_On3*, where each value is part of a "*WHEN*" clause associated with a sequence of statements. For example, if the case statement executes with *Currstate* being *S_On1*, then the selected sequence of statements for execution would be "*x <= '1'; Nextstate <= S_On2;*". Describing an FSM involves associating with each case statement choice two things: the actions of the corresponding state, followed by statements describing the transitions from a state. For example, state *S_Off*'s action is "*x <= '0';*". *S_Off*'s next state is computed using an *IF-THEN-ELSE* statement such that if *b* is '0', the next state is set to *S_off*, whereas if *b*

```
ENTITY LaserTimer IS
    PORT (b: IN std_logic;
          x: OUT std_logic;
          Clk, Rst: IN std_logic );
END LaserTimer;

ARCHITECTURE Beh OF LaserTimer IS
    TYPE Statetype IS
        (S_Off, S_On1, S_On2, S_On3);
    SIGNAL Currstate, Nextstate: Statetype;
BEGIN
    CombLogic: PROCESS (Currstate, b)
    BEGIN

    . . .

    END PROCESS CombLogic;

    StateReg: PROCESS (Clk)
    BEGIN

    . . .

    END PROCESS StateReg;

END Beh;
```

Figure 3.11 Two-process FSM behavioral description approach.

is '*1*', the next state is *S_On1*, corresponding to the transitions leaving *S_Off* in the FSM diagram in Figure 3.10(a).

The *StateReg* process is shown in Figure 3.13. The process is similar to the register process introduced in Section 3.1. The process is sensitive to the clock, and first checks if the clock change was a rising edge. If so, the register checks if the reset input is '*1*', in which case the process sets the current state signal to the FSM's initial state, or *S_Off*. If the reset input is not '*1*', then the register simply stores its data input, namely *Nextstate*, into *Currstate*.

Note that the two processes are similar to a two-component approach, except that the interfaces are not specified using ports, but rather using shared signals.

One could instead describe an FSM using a single process. That process would have the same form as the process in Figure 3.13, with the *ELSE*'s single statement replaced by the complete *CASE* statement of Figure 3.12. However, a two-process approach has two advantages. First, some automatic circuit creation tools may not create a simple state register and combinational logic implementation from the process of the single-process approach, instead creating a more complex circuit. Second, the single-process approach becomes complicated when describing a Mealy FSM, which is a type of FSM whose outputs may change asynchronously when inputs change. Such asynchronous behavior is easily captured in the two process approach, whose combinational logic process is already asynchronous. However, in the single-process approach, the single process would need to

```
  ...
     SIGNAL Currstate, Nextstate: Statetype;
BEGIN
   CombLogic: PROCESS (Currstate, b)
   BEGIN
      CASE Currstate IS
         WHEN S_Off =>
            x <= '0';
            IF (b = '0') THEN
               Nextstate <= S_Off;
            ELSE
               Nextstate <= S_On1;
            END IF;
         WHEN S_On1 =>
            x <= '1';
            Nextstate <= S_On2;
         WHEN S_On2 =>
            x <= '1';
            Nextstate <= S_On3;
         WHEN S_On3 =>
            x <= '1';
            Nextstate <= S_Off;
      END CASE;
   END PROCESS CombLogic;
  ...
```

Figure 3.12 FSM's *CombLogic* process.

```
  ...
   StateReg: PROCESS (Clk)
   BEGIN
      IF (Clk = '1' AND Clk'EVENT) THEN
         IF (Rst = '1') THEN
            Currstate <= S_Off;
         ELSE
            Currstate <= Nextstate;
         END IF;
      END IF;
   END PROCESS StateReg;
  ...
```

Figure 3.13 FSM's *StateReg* process.

be extended to be sensitive to both the clock and to inputs, and to have part of the code as synchronous and the other part as asynchronous, resulting in a rather awkward description that may not correspond directly to the register and combinational logic implementation model for an FSM.

⊓⊔⊓

[SIMUL] ASSERTION STATEMENTS IN TESTBENCHES

Figure 3.14 shows the key parts of a basic testbench for the earlier FSM example. Like the register testbench from Section 3.1, the FSM's testbench has two processes, one to generate the clock input, and the other to generate test vectors. The vector process first initializes the FSM to the FSM's initial state, by setting *Rst_s* to *'1'*, and then waiting for a rising clock edge. Following good convention, the process also sets the input *b_s* to a specific value, in this case *'0'*, during initialization. Next (after waiting 5 ns before setting new test vectors), the process provides a sequence of values on the FSM's input *b_s* for a number of clock cycles. Notice that the testbench doesn't explicitly set the inputs on every clock cycle, relying instead on the fact that the inputs maintain their previous values. Some would argue that better practice involves setting every input explicitly on every cycle. For components with only a few inputs, explicitly setting every input may be feasible, but large numbers of inputs may result in such explicit setting yielding too many lines of code.

The waveforms resulting from simulating the testbench appear in Figure 3.15. We can manually examine these waveforms to determine whether the FSM behaves as expected for the given input vectors. We see that *b_s* becomes *'1'* for one clock cycle, and we know

```
    ...
    ClkProcess: PROCESS
    BEGIN
        Clk_s <= '0';
        WAIT FOR 10 NS;
        Clk_s <= '1';
        WAIT FOR 10 NS;
    END PROCESS ClkProcess;

    VectorProcess: PROCESS
    BEGIN
        Rst_s <= '1';
        b_s <= '0';
        WAIT UNTIL Clk_s='1' AND Clk_s'EVENT;
        WAIT FOR 5 NS;
        Rst_s <= '0';
        WAIT UNTIL Clk_s='1' AND Clk_s'EVENT;
        WAIT FOR 5 NS;
        b_s <= '1';
        WAIT UNTIL Clk_s='1' AND Clk_s'EVENT;
        WAIT FOR 5 NS;
        b_s <= '0';
        WAIT UNTIL Clk_s='1' AND Clk_s'EVENT;
        WAIT UNTIL Clk_s='1' AND Clk_s'EVENT;
        WAIT UNTIL Clk_s='1' AND Clk_s'EVENT;
        WAIT;
    END PROCESS VectorProcess;

END TBarch;
```

Figure 3.14 Basic testbench for an FSM.

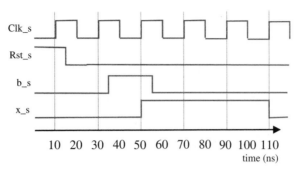

Figure 3.15 FSM's *StateReg* process.

from Figure 3.10(a) that the FSM should output $x\_s=1$ for three clock cycles after such an occurrence. We see in the waveform that x_s indeed becomes '1' for three cycles after b_s became '1', thus increasing our confidence that the FSM description is correct.

Examining waveforms manually in the above manner is tedious and prone to errors, especially when the testbench generates thousands of test vectors rather than just a few. A more automated testbench approach, shown in Figure 3.16, makes use of assertion statements. An ***assertion statement*** checks if a condition is true, reporting an error if not. The testbench in Figure 3.16 has its first assertion statement just after initializing the FSM. Because the FSM should set output x_s to '0' in the initial state S_Off, the assertion statement begins with "*ASSERT* x_s = '0';". If x_s is indeed '0', execution proceeds to the next statement. However, if x_s is not '0', then the next part of the assert statement, "*REPORT "Reset failed";*" would be printed out by the simulator. Some simulators will also print out the line in the testbench where the assertion statement appears. The report part of the assertion statement is optional; if that part is absent, the default report string "*Assertion violation*" will be printed.

Assert statements also allow for an optional ***severity clause*** to be included at the end of the assert statement, using the keyword "*SEVERITY*". The severity clause indicates the importance of the assertion failure. Possible severity values are "*ERROR*", "*WARNING*", and "*NOTE*", with "*ERROR*" being the default value. The severity clause provides additional information to the simulator, allowing the simulator to decide how to report the error. For example, a simulator might halt simulation if an assertion "*ERROR*" occurs but may instead continue simulation if an assertion "*WARNING*" occurs. This behavior is often configurable within a simulator and can be helpful when debugging. Halting the simulator in the event of an assert "*ERROR*" may allow a designer to quickly find the error without having to search through the simulation waveform to find the error.

Assertion statements provide a way for a testbench to check itself, thus relieving the designer from the tedious task of manually examining lengthy waveforms to determine whether those waveforms match expected behavior.

```
...
VectorProcess: PROCESS
BEGIN
   Rst_s <= '1';
   b_s <= '0';
   WAIT UNTIL Clk_s='1' AND Clk_s'EVENT;
   WAIT FOR 5 NS;
   ASSERT x_s = '0' REPORT "Reset failed";
   Rst_s <= '0';
   WAIT UNTIL Clk_s='1' AND Clk_s'EVENT;
   WAIT FOR 5 NS;
   b_s <= '1';
   WAIT UNTIL Clk_s='1' AND Clk_s'EVENT;
   WAIT FOR 5 NS;
   b_s <= '0';
   ASSERT x_s = '1' REPORT "First x=1 failed";
   WAIT UNTIL Clk_s='1' AND Clk_s'EVENT;
   WAIT FOR 5 NS;
   ASSERT x_s = '1' REPORT "Second x=1 failed";
   WAIT UNTIL Clk_s='1' AND Clk_s'EVENT;
   WAIT FOR 5 NS;
   ASSERT x_s = '1' REPORT "Third x=1 failed";
   WAIT UNTIL Clk_s='1' AND Clk_s'EVENT;
   WAIT FOR 5 NS;
   ASSERT x_s = '0' REPORT "Final x=0 failed";
   WAIT;
END PROCESS VectorProcess;
...
```

Figure 3.16 ASSERT-based testbench for an FSM. (Note: vertical space between vectors would improve readability, but is omitted here for space reasons.)

3.3 TOP-DOWN DESIGN—FSMS TO CONTROLLER STRUCTURE

As discussed in the previous chapter, a top-down design approach involves first capturing behavior and simulating, and then creating structure and simulating again. The previous section showed how to capture FSM behavior and simulate that behavior. This section proceeds with the top-down approach, to create structure and simulate again.

Figure 3.17 illustrates the steps involved in converting an FSM to a structural controller implementation of that FSM. The first step creates the architecture, consisting of a two-bit state register, and combinational logic, as in Figure 3.17(a). The next step encodes the states using unique bit representations, as shown in Figure 3.17(b). The encoding results in the state table of Figure 3.17(c). From this state table, one can derive the combinational logic equations of Figure 3.17(d). Implementing those equations as a circuit inside the combinational logic block of Figure 3.17(a) would complete the controller design.

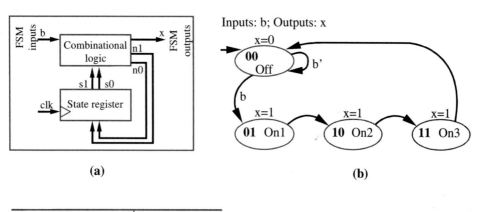

(a)

(b)

	Inputs			Outputs		
	s1	s0	b	x	n1	n0
Off	0	0	0	0	0	0
	0	0	1	0	0	1
On1	0	1	0	1	1	0
	0	1	1	1	1	0
On2	1	0	0	1	1	1
	1	0	1	1	1	1
On3	1	1	0	1	0	0
	1	1	1	1	0	0

(c)

$$x = s1 + s0$$
$$n1 = s1's0 + s1s0'$$
$$n0 = s1's0'b + s1s0'$$

(d)

Figure 3.17 Top-down FSM to controller design: (a) architecture, (b) encoded states, (c) state table, (d) combinational logic.

Figure 3.18 shows the controller description of the FSM. This description differs from the original FSM description shown in Figure 3.11, Figure 3.12, and Figure 3.13, in several ways.

First, *Statetype* is no longer defined using a type declaration that enumerates four states, but instead using a subtype declaration that represents a 2-bit value. A *subtype declaration* declares a new subtype that is a restricted form of a previously-defined type (or subtype). In this case, *Statetype* is declared to be a restricted form of *std_logic_vector* in which the vector range is specifically restricted to be "*1 DOWNTO 0*".

Second, the encoding "*00*" for the initial state S_Off is declared as a constant. A *constant declaration* declares an identifier as a given type and sets that identifier to the specified value (using "*:=*" to assign that value), such that the identifier's value cannot be changed after the declaration. In this example, the statement "*CONSTANT S_Off : Statetype := "00";*" defines the identifier S_Off of type *Statetype* and sets S_Off's value to "*00*".

```
LIBRARY ieee;
USE ieee.std_logic_1164.ALL;

ENTITY LaserTimer IS
    PORT (b: IN std_logic;
          x: OUT std_logic;
          Clk, Rst: IN std_logic );
END LaserTimer;

ARCHITECTURE Struct OF LaserTimer IS
    SUBTYPE Statetype IS std_logic_vector(1 DOWNTO 0);
    CONSTANT S_Off : Statetype := "00";
    SIGNAL Currstate, Nextstate: Statetype;
BEGIN
    CombLogic: PROCESS (Currstate, b)
    BEGIN
        x <= Currstate(1) OR Currstate(0);
        Nextstate(1) <= (NOT(Currstate(1)) AND Currstate(0))
                     OR (Currstate(1) AND NOT(Currstate(0)));
        Nextstate(0) <= (NOT(Currstate(1)) AND NOT(Currstate(0)) AND b)
                     OR (Currstate(1) AND NOT(Currstate(0)));
    END PROCESS CombLogic;

    StateReg: PROCESS (Clk)
    BEGIN
        IF (Clk = '1' AND Clk'EVENT) THEN
            IF (Rst = '1') THEN
                Currstate <= S_Off;
            ELSE
                Currstate <= Nextstate;
            END IF;
        END IF;
    END PROCESS StateReg;

END Struct;
```

Figure 3.18 Controller description for earlier-introduced FSM.

Third, the combinational logic process now directly models the combinational functions using equations, rather than indirectly modeling those functions using a case statement. Note how much less the equations convey the intended system behavior to the reader, compared to the case statement, even though the equations are more compact.

The controller description has exactly the same input and output ports as did the earlier FSM description. The controller description can be simulated using the same testbench as in Section 3.2, resulting in the same waveforms as in Figure 3.15.

Although we said the controller description represented "structure," notice that the combinational logic process is actually a behavioral description of the combinational logic, rather than a structural description. Such behavioral description of combinational logic was covered in Chapter 2. That combinational behavior could be further refined, again using top-down design approach, to create a structural connection of gates for the combinational logic. Note that the top-down design process may be repeated for different parts of a design, until finally reaching a structural circuit consisting of low-level components.

[SYNTH] COMMON PITFALL

Not assigning output signals in every state

A common mistake when describing FSMs is to not assign every FSM output in every state. Failing to assign an output means the output's value will be remembered, rather than updated, by the process during a particular clock cycle. That remembered value means the output has storage, and thus that the output is not just determined by the present state as is intended. Simulation may not unveil the storage if test vectors are not thorough enough, but synthesis tools will either refuse to synthesize such a circuit, report a warning during synthesis, or generate a circuit that behaves different from a designer's expectations.

Many experienced designers avoid this problem using one of two methods. One method is to ensure every output is assigned in every state, perhaps by cut-and-pasting a sequence of assignment statements, which includes every output, into every alternative of a case statement, with each sequence requiring completion with a specific assigned values.

Another method is to initially assign every output to a default value before the case statement, as illustrated in Figure 3.19. If an output does not get assigned by a case statement alternative during execution of the case statement, the initially assigned value will be the actual assigned value for that output during that execution of the process. However, if that output does get assigned in a case statement alternative, then that assignment overrides the initial assignment.

```
CombLogic: PROCESS (Currstate, b)
BEGIN
    x <= '0';
    CASE Currstate IS
        WHEN S_Off =>
            x <= '0';
            IF (b = '0') THEN
                Nextstate <= S_Off;
            ELSE
                Nextstate <= S_On1;
            END IF;
        WHEN S_On1 =>
            x <= '1';
            Nextstate <= S_On2;
        WHEN S_On2 =>
            x <= '1';
            Nextstate <= S_On3;
        WHEN S_On3 =>
            x <= '1';
            Nextstate <= S_Off;
    END CASE;
END PROCESS CombLogic;
```

Figure 3.19 Initializing FSM outputs.

In Figure 3.19, the FSM's output x is initialized to '0'. If process execution executes any of the S_On case statement alternatives, the assignment of x to '1' will override the earlier assignment to '0'. If instead process execution executes the S_Off alternative, x will be set to '0'.

Notice that the assignment to '0' in S_Off's statements is redundant with the assignment to '0' during initialization, and could be eliminated. However, it may be best to leave that assignment there to make the behavior of state S_Off entirely clear.

The initialization method of avoiding the pitfall is useful when an FSM has many outputs, because the method improves the readability of each case statement alternative. Only the outputs that are assigned a different value from the default, or for which a designer wishes to clearly show being assigned a value in a state, need be included in each case statement alternative. Figure 3.20 illustrates such improved readability. Figure 3.20(a) shows all outputs assigned in every state. Figure 3.20(b) shows only the relevant output assignments for each—clearly, state S assigns b to '1', and state T assigns c to '1'. Note that such output initialization can be used to support the common simplifying FSM notation that assumes every output not explicitly assigned in a state is implicitly assigned '0', as illustrated in the figure.

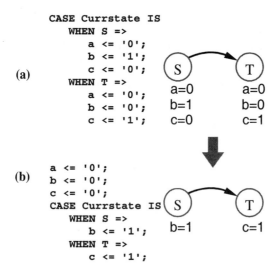

Figure 3.20 Initializing FSM outputs can improve readability:
(a) without initialization, (b) with initialization.

3.4 MORE SIMULATION CONCEPTS

[SIMUL] THE SIMULATION CYCLE

It can be instructive to learn how a simulator executes an HDL description to generate waveforms. This section will highlight how a simulator would execute the example description in Figure 3.21. HDL simulation is complex; this section only provides some key highlights.

The example has three user-defined signals: Q, Clk, and S. Note that ports are signals, which is why Q is included in the list of signals. The example also has three processes: $P1$, $P2$, and $P3$. The job of the simulator will be to determine values for the three signals over time. The simulator will accomplish this job by repeatedly executing and suspending the three processes, which assign values to the signals.

```
LIBRARY ieee;
USE ieee.std_logic_1164.ALL;

ENTITY SimEx1 IS
    PORT (Q: OUT std_logic );
END SimEx1;

ARCHITECTURE SimEx1Arch OF SimEx1 IS
    SIGNAL Clk, S: std_logic;
BEGIN
    P1: PROCESS
    BEGIN
        Clk <= '0';
        WAIT FOR 10 NS;
        Clk <= '1';
        WAIT FOR 10 NS;
    END PROCESS P1;
```

Same as:

```
P2: PROCESS(S)          P2: PROCESS
BEGIN                   BEGIN
    Q <= NOT(S);            Q <= NOT(S);
END PROCESS P2;             WAIT ON S;
                        END PROCESS P2;
```

```
    P3: PROCESS
    BEGIN
        WAIT UNTIL Clk='1' AND Clk'EVENT;
        S <= '1';
        WAIT UNTIL Clk='1' AND Clk'EVENT;
        S <= '0';
        WAIT;
    END PROCESS P3;
END SimEx1Arch;
```

Figure 3.21 Example to demonstrate simulation concepts.

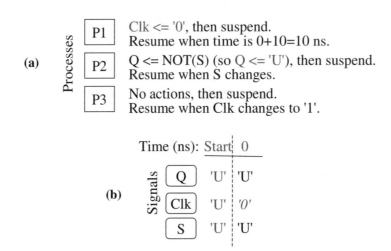

Figure 3.22 Simulation initialization: (a) Process execution and suspension, (b) signal values before/after initialization.

A process **suspends** whenever the process execution reaches a *WAIT* statement. Notice that process *P2* does not have a *WAIT* statement, but instead has a sensitivity list. A process with a sensitivity list is equivalent to a process that does not have a sensitivity list, but that instead has a *WAIT* statement as the process' last statement, where that *WAIT* statement waits on changes of the signals that were in the original sensitivity list. Such a process is shown in Figure 3.21. The **WAIT ON** form of a *WAIT* statement has a list of signals to which the statement is sensitive. The process suspends upon reaching that statement, and resumes only when one (or more) of the signals in the sensitivity list changes. We'll thus consider that form of *P2*.

The first step of simulation is initialization. At the start of simulation, all signals have the value *undefined* (*'U'*), as shown in Figure 3.22(b) under the heading *Start*. The initialization step then executes each process, one at a time, until each process suspends due to a wait statement. As shown in Figure 3.22(a), the simulator will execute process P1's first statement "*Clk <= '0';*" and then suspend at the statement "*WAIT FOR 10 ns;*". The simulator will note that this process should resume execution 10 ns after the present simulation time of 0 ns, meaning *P1* should resume at time 0 ns + 10 ns = 10 ns. The simulator will then execute process *P2*'s first statement "*Q <= NOT(S);*", which means *Q* should get the value of undefined because *S* is undefined, and the process will then suspend at the statement "*WAIT ON S;*". The simulator will note that this process should resume execution when *S* changes. Finally, the simulator will execute P3 but will immediately suspend, due to that process' first statement being "*WAIT UNTIL Clk='1' AND Clk'EVENT;*". The simulator will note that this process should resume when *Clk* changes to *'1'*. After initialization, the signal values will be those shown for time 0 ns in Figure 3.22(b).

Once the simulator completes the initialization and has initial values for time 0 ns, the simulator will continue simulation by repeatedly executing the simulation cycle. During each *simulation cycle*, the simulator advances simulation time to the next time at which a process (or processes) resumes, and executes the resumed process until the process suspends. In this case, the simulator will advance time to 10 ns, at which time process *P1* resumes, as shown in Figure 3.23(a). The simulator resumes *P1,* executes the statement "*Clk <= '1';*", and then suspends at the following statement "*WAIT FOR 10 ns;*". As before, the simulator notes that this process should resume execution 10 ns after the present simulation time of 10 ns, meaning *P1* should resume again at time 20 ns.

The simulator then advances execution to the next time at which a process resumes. Remember that the simulator previously noted that process *P3* should resume when *Clk* changes to '*1*'. During execution of process *P1*, the simulator updated the value of *Clk* signal to '*1*' and should now resume process *P3*. Thus, to execute *P3*, the simulator "advances" time to 10 ns. In this case, the simulator may "advances" the simulation time to the current time (i.e., advancing from 10 ns to 10 ns), indicating that additional processes need to be executed at this current time. A simulation cycle whose simulated time is actu-

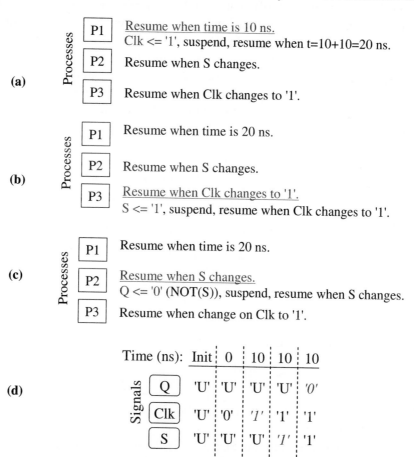

Figure 3.23 Simulation execution: (a) Process execution and suspension, (b) signal values during simulation execution.

ally the same as that of the previous simulation cycle is known as a ***delta cycle***. After advancing the simulation time to the current time, the simulator executes *P3* by executing the statement "*S <= '1';*" and then suspends the process at the following statement "*WAIT UNTIL Clk='1' AND Clk'EVENT;*". The simulator notes that this process should resume again when *Clk* changes to '*1*'.

Process *P2* was previously suspended at the statement "*WAIT ON S;*". While executing process *P3*, the simulator updated the value of S from '*U*' to '*1*' and now needs to execute process *P2*. To do so, the simulator will again advance the simulation time to the current time of 10 ns, meaning the simulator will execute another delta cycle. The simulator executes process *P2*, as shown in Figure 3.23(c). The simulator will execute the statement "*Q <= NOT(S);*" and assign a value of '*0*' to the signal *Q*. The simulator will then suspend process *P2* at the statement "*WAIT ON S;*" and note that process *P2* should resume execution when *S* changes again.

After several simulation cycles at time 10 ns, the signal values will be the last values shown for time 10 ns in Figure 3.23(d). Note that during this simulation, the simulator will keep track of the signals' values as the simulator executes each process, but the output waveforms will only show the final signal values at the end of the current time.

The simulator will advance time to 20 ns and continue executing simulation cycles, until the user-specified simulation time is reached. The signal values determined during simulation will translate to the output simulation waveform, as shown in Figure 3.24. Notice how the waveform values correspond to the final values determined during simulation for each simulation time.

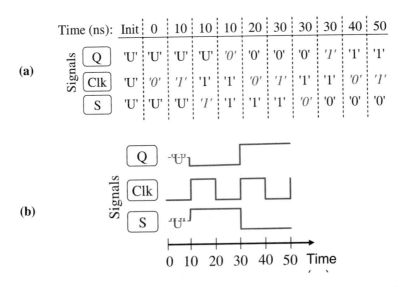

Figure 3.24 Simulation results: (a) Signal values over time as computed during simulation, (b) waveforms derived from those signal values.

[SIMUL] SIGNAL DRIVERS AND EVENTS

In describing the simulation cycle of a simulator, we assumed that updates to a signal's value happened immediately. In fact, signal assignments within a simulation cycle will not update the signal's value immediately. Instead, a signal assignment will change the projected value of the signal. The ***projected value*** of a signal is the value a simulator determines should be assigned to the signal at the beginning of a future simulation cycle. The signal's value will be updated with the projected value during the beginning of the next simulation cycle. We need to revise the previous explanation of a simulation cycle to include updating the signals' values. During this revised explanation of a simulation cycle, the simulator advances simulation time to the next time at which a process (or processes) will resume, updates the values of any active signal, and executes the resumed process until the process suspends.

It is important to consider the implication of this revised explanation of a simulation cycle and projected signal values. One implication is that the execution order of processes during a simulation cycle does not matter. For example, consider the two processes, *Process1* and *Process2*, shown in Figure 3.25. Assume that both of those processes are resumed during the same simulation cycle, and assume that *B* is '*0*'. The simulator will resume *Process1*, execute the statement "*B <= NOT(B);*", update the projected value of *B* to '*1*', and suspend the process. Within the same simulation cycle, the simulator will resume *Process2*, execute the statement "*A <= B;*", and update the projected value of *A* to '*0*'. Note that during that simulation cycle, the current value of *B* will be '*0*' for both processes. Thus, at the start of the next simulation cycle, *B* will be updated to '*1*', and *A* will be updated to '*0*', not to '*1*'.

Assume B is '0'.
Process1:
```
B <= NOT(B);
```
Process2:
```
A <= B;
```
A will be '0', not '1'.

Figure 3.25 Projected values: Signals values are updated at the beginning of the next simulation cycle.

In addition, the execution order of assignments to different signals within a process does not matter. Consider the two alternative processes, *Process3a* and *Process3b*, shown in Figure 3.26. These two processes consist of the same two assignment statements, "$C <=$ $NOT(C);$" and "$D <= C;$", but with opposite ordering of the two statements. Assume the current value of C is '0'. Regardless of which process is used, after executing the process, C will be '1' and D will be '0'. Each assignment statement will use the current value, not the projected value, of C to determine the next values for C and D. The assignment statements do not modify the current value of C or D, but rather the projected value, and both processes will have the same behavior even though the assignments to C and D have different orders within the two processes. For example, when executing *Process3a*, the simulator will execute the statement "$C <= NOT(C);$" and assign '1' to the projected value of C. When executing the following statement, "$D <= C;$", the simulator will use the current value of C, not the projected value, and assign '0' to the projected value of D.

Process3a:
```
C <= NOT(C);
D <= C;
```
←— Same —→
Process3b:
```
D <= C;
C <= NOT(C);
```

Figure 3.26 Projected values: Order of assignments to different signals within a process does not matter.

Projected signal values further imply that later signal assignments to a particular signal within a process have precedence over earlier assignments to that same signal. Considering the process example in Figure 3.27, the simulator will execute the statement "$E <= '0';$" and update the projected value of E to '0'. However, the simulator then executes the statement "$E <= '1';$" further down in the process, and thus the simulator will replace E's projected value of '0' with '1'. The next value of E will thus be '1', not '0'. Further recall the FSM example in Figure 3.19. That FSM's implementation took advantage of the fact that later output assignments (the assignment within a state's WHEN clause) have precedence over earlier assignments (the default output assignment before the CASE statement).

Process4:
```
E <= '0';
...
E <= '1';
```

Figure 3.27 Projected values: Later signal assignments have precedence over earlier assignment

3.5 RESETS

Reset behavior is the behavior of a register (or other sequential element, like a flip-flop) that occurs when a special reset input is asserted. For example, the register described in Figure 3.2 included reset behavior that cleared the register to 0s when an input *Rst* equaled '*1*', and the register described in Figure 3.13 had reset behavior that initialized the register to the value "*S_Off*" when an input Rst equaled '*1*'. Good design practice dictates having a defined reset behavior for every register in a design, thus ensuring that a design always starts from the same starting point. Reset behavior should always have priority over normal register operation.

Reset behavior usually clears a register to 0s, but may instead initialize a register to a specific non-zero value, such as when initializing a controller's state register to the encoding of the initial state of an FSM. A system's reset input is typically asserted externally at the start of operation of a sequential circuit, such as when a chip is first powered on. However, resets can also occur during circuit operation, perhaps due to a detected failure, due to a user request, or for some other reason.

The previous examples of Figure 3.2 and Figure 3.13 used a reset technique known as synchronous reset. A ***synchronous reset*** is a reset that, when asserted, only takes effect at the next rising clock. Figure 3.28(b) shows the behavior of the synchronous reset of the register described in Figure 3.2, whose description is shown again in Figure 3.28(a) for convenience. The setting of *Rst* to '*1*' has no effect until a rising clock edge arrives, at which time the reset of the register to 0s takes place.

A second reset technique is known as asynchronous reset. An ***asynchronous reset*** is a reset that takes effect almost immediately after being asserted, independently from the clock signal. Figure 3.28(c) provides a description of the same register from Figure 3.28(a) except that the register's reset behavior is now described to be asynchronous. To achieve an asynchronous reset, the description includes *Rst* in the sensitivity list of the process—if *Rst* were omitted, the process would only evaluate the *Rst* signal when the clock signal changed, and thus the reset would be synchronous. The description also places the reset behavior outside of the IF statement that detects a rising clock edge. For the reset behavior to have priority over normal operation, the check for *Rst* equal to '*1*' must occur before the check for a rising clock, and the check for a rising clock must be an ELSIF part rather than a separate IF statement. Figure 3.28(d) illustrates the behavior of this asynchronous reset. The setting of *Rst* to '*1*' has an effect almost immediately, causing the reset of the register to 0s.

```
LIBRARY ieee;
USE ieee.std_logic_1164.ALL;

ENTITY Reg4 IS
    PORT (I: IN std_logic_vector(3 DOWNTO 0);
          Q: OUT std_logic_vector(3 DOWNTO 0);
          Clk, Rst: IN std_logic );
END Reg4;

ARCHITECTURE Beh OF Reg4 IS
BEGIN
    PROCESS (Clk)
    BEGIN
        IF (Clk = '1' AND Clk'EVENT) THEN
            IF (Rst = '1') THEN
                Q <= "0000";
            ELSE
                Q <= I;
            END IF;
        END IF;
    END PROCESS;
END Beh;
```
(a)

```
LIBRARY ieee;
USE ieee.std_logic_1164.ALL;

ENTITY Reg4 IS
    PORT (I: IN std_logic_vector(3 DOWNTO 0);
          Q: OUT std_logic_vector(3 DOWNTO 0);
          Clk, Rst: IN std_logic );
END Reg4;

ARCHITECTURE BehAsyRst OF Reg4 IS
BEGIN
    PROCESS (Clk, Rst)
    BEGIN
        IF (Rst = '1') THEN
            Q <= "0000";
        ELSIF (Clk = '1' AND Clk'EVENT) THEN
            Q <= I;
        END IF;
    END PROCESS;
END BehAsyRst;
```
(c)

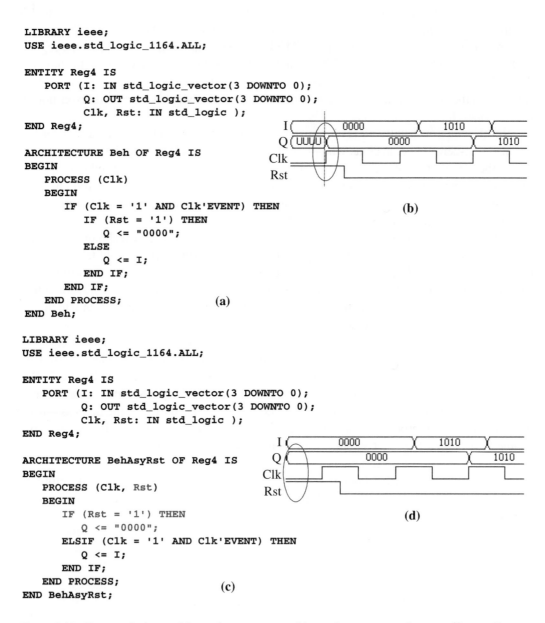

(b)

(d)

Figure 3.28 Reset techniques: (a) synchronous reset, (b) synchronous reset has no effect until next rising clock, (c) asynchronous reset, (d) asynchronous reset has effect almost immediately, independently from the clock.

```
    ...
        StateReg: PROCESS (Clk)
        BEGIN
          IF (Clk = '1' AND Clk'EVENT) THEN
            IF (Rst = '1') THEN
(a)           Currstate <= S_Off;
            ELSE
              Currstate <= Nextstate;
            END IF;
          END IF;
        END PROCESS StateReg;
    ...


    ...
        StateReg: PROCESS (Clk, Rst)
        BEGIN
          IF (Rst = '1') THEN
            Currstate <= S_Off;
(b)       ELSIF (Clk = '1' AND Clk'EVENT) THEN
            Currstate <= Nextstate;
          END IF;
        END PROCESS StateReg;
    ...
```

Figure 3.29 FSM's *StateReg* process with: (a) synchronous reset, (b) asynchronous reset.

The state register process from Figure 3.13, shown again in Figure 3.29(a) for convenience, could have also been described to use an asynchronous reset rather than a synchronous reset, as shown in Figure 3.29(b).

Whether designers should use synchronous or asynchronous resets is a hotly debated subject in the design community. Each approach has pros and cons. For example, asynchronous resets can reset a circuit even if the clock is not functioning. On the other hand, synchronous resets may make timing analysis a bit easier. The debate cannot be settled here. The important thing is to be consistent in the use of resets throughout a design. All registers should have defined reset behavior that takes priority over normal register behavior, and that reset behavior should all be synchronous reset or should all be asynchronous reset. This book will use synchronous resets in the remaining examples.

3.6 DESCRIBING SAFE FSMS

A *safe FSM* is an FSM whose definition is such that if the FSM were to ever enter an illegal state, the FSM would transition to a legal state. Figure 3.30(a) shows an unsafe FSM. The FSM uses a two-bit state encoding but has only three states, resulting in one illegal state encoded as "*11*". Such an illegal state is also called an *unreachable* state. In theory, an illegal state can never be reached during operation of the FSM. In practice, however, such a state may be reached due to a circuit error. For example, severe electrical noise could result in a bit change from 0 to 1 or vice versa. If an illegal state is reached, the FSM's behavior is undefined. A circuit synthesized for that FSM could conceivably get stuck in such an illegal state (or begin transitioning among illegal states).

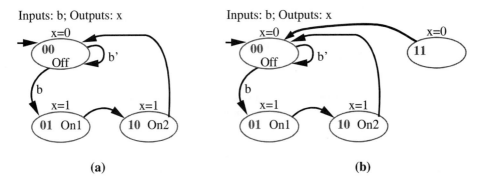

(a)   **(b)**

Figure 3.30   Unsafe versus safe FSMs: (a) Unsafe FSM may get stuck in an undefined state ("*11*"), (b) Safe FSM explicitly transitions from undefined states back to a defined state.

Figure 3.30(b) shows a safe version of the same FSM, in which the illegal state is explicitly included in the FSM. That state transitions to state *Off*, while outputting *x=0*. Although the state looks odd due to having no transitions leading to the state, remember that the state can only be reached due to a circuit error.

Figure 3.31(a) shows a description of an unsafe FSM in VHDL. Only the legal states appear in the description. Synthesis of a controller from this FSM might result in the creation of an unsafe controller. Some synthesis tools support a "safe" synthesis option that automatically converts an unsafe FSM description into a safe FSM during synthesis.

In contrast, Figure 3.31(b) explicitly describes safe FSM. The description makes use of an OTHERS choice in a case statement. A case statement may contain one *OTHERS* choice, which must be the last choice of the case statement, and which is chosen only if none of the earlier choices match.

Note that the OTHERS approach enables safe FSM description even before the FSM states have been encoded.

Good practice dictates including an OTHERS choice in all state machines. One might believe that the OTHERS choice is not needed if the number of states is a power of two. However, before states have been encoded, there is no guarantee that a synthesis tool will

...

```
    CombLogic: PROCESS (Currstate, b)
    BEGIN
        CASE Currstate IS
            WHEN S_Off =>
                x <= '0';
                IF (b = '0') THEN
                    Nextstate <= S_Off;
                ELSE
                    Nextstate <= S_On1;
                END IF;
            WHEN S_On1 =>
                x <= '1';
                Nextstate <= S_On2;
            WHEN S_On2 =>
                x <= '1';
                Nextstate <= S_Off;
        END CASE;
    END PROCESS CombLogic;
...

                            (a)
```

```
...
    CombLogic: PROCESS (Currstate, b)
    BEGIN
        CASE Currstate IS
            WHEN S_Off =>
                x <= '0';
                IF (b = '0') THEN
                    Nextstate <= S_Off;
                ELSE
                    Nextstate <= S_On1;
                END IF;
            WHEN S_On1 =>
                x <= '1';
                Nextstate <= S_On2;
            WHEN S_On2 =>
                x <= '1';
                Nextstate <= S_Off;
            WHEN OTHERS =>
                x <= '0';
                Nextstate <= S_Off;
        END CASE;
    END PROCESS CombLogic;
...

                            (b)
```

Figure 3.31 Unsafe versus safe FSM descriptions: (a) Unsafe FSM description only lists legal states, (b) Safe FSM description uses OTHERS choice in CASE statement to cover illegal states, which all would transition back to S_Off.

encode states using the minimum number of bits. The tool might, for example, encode states using a one-hot encoding, which uses as many bits as there are states in the FSM. Such an encoding will have numerous illegal states. Using an OTHERS choice ensures that an illegal state will have a defined transition back to a legal state. Thus, including an OTHERS choice is likely wise for all state machines.

CHAPTER 4

Datapath Components

4.1 MULTIFUNCTION REGISTERS

The previous chapter showed a register that had only a reset control input. A more general register may have more control inputs, such as load, shift right, and shift left control inputs, along with data inputs when shifting right or left. Such a multi-function register appears in Figure 4.1(a), with the register's operations appearing in Figure 4.1(b).

Describing a multifunction register could be done structurally, by connecting four flip-flops, four muxes, and combinational logic to convert the control inputs into mux select inputs.

The register can instead be described behaviorally, as shown in Figure 4.2. The *IF* statement maintains the priorities among the control inputs of Figure 4.1(b), through the ordering of the *ELSIF* parts. *Rst* has highest priority, then *Ld*, then *Shr*, and finally *Shl*.

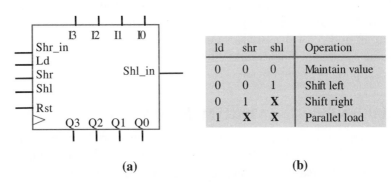

ld	shr	shl	Operation
0	0	0	Maintain value
0	0	1	Shift left
0	1	X	Shift right
1	X	X	Parallel load

(a)   (b)

Figure 4.1 A multifunction register: (a) block diagram, (b) operation table.

```
LIBRARY ieee;
USE ieee.std_logic_1164.ALL;

ENTITY MfReg4 IS
   PORT (I: IN std_logic_vector(3 DOWNTO 0);
         Q: OUT std_logic_vector(3 DOWNTO 0);
         Ld, Shr, Shl, Shr_in, Shl_in: IN std_logic;
         Clk, Rst: IN std_logic );
END MfReg4;

ARCHITECTURE Beh OF MfReg4 IS
   SIGNAL R: std_logic_vector(3 DOWNTO 0);
BEGIN
   PROCESS (Clk)
   BEGIN
      IF (Clk = '1' AND Clk'EVENT) THEN
         IF (Rst = '1') THEN
            R <= "0000";
         ELSIF (Ld = '1') THEN
            R <= I;
         ELSIF (Shr = '1') THEN
            R(3) <= Shr_in; R(2) <= R(3);
            R(1) <= R(2); R(0) <= R(1);
         ELSIF (Shl = '1') THEN
            R(0) <= Shl_in; R(1) <= R(2);
            R(2) <= R(1); R(3) <= R(2);
         END IF;
      END IF;
   END PROCESS;

   Q <= R;

END Beh;
```

Figure 4.2 Multifunction register behavioral description.

When *Shr* is *'1'*, the shift is accomplished using four statements that assign each bit to the location on the right. Recall that each signal assignment statement results in an update of the signal value at the beginning of the next simulation cycle, rather than immediately, and thus the order of those assignment statements in the description does not matter.

CONCURRENT SIGNAL ASSIGNMENT STATEMENT

In the register description of Section 3.1, the output port Q, being a signal, was used for the register's storage. However, the description in Figure 4.2 uses a signal R for storage. The reason for using a distinct signal is that the shift operations require that the description *read* the stored value, but an output port, such as port Q in Figure 4.2, may not be read.

Because the register should output the stored value on port Q, a mechanism is needed to copy signal R's value to port Q at all times. The description in Figure

4.2 therefore includes the statement "*Q <= R;*" near the bottom of the description. However, note that the statement *is not contained within the process*. A signal assignment statement appearing outside a process in an architecture is known as a concurrent signal assignment statement. A **concurrent signal assignment statement** is shorthand notation for another process, executing concurrently with any other processes, and being equivalent to a process that has the appropriate sensitivity list and a single signal assignment statement. The concurrent signal assignment statement "*Q <= R;*' is equivalent to the following process:

```
PROCESS(R)
BEGIN
    Q <= R;
END PROCESS;
```

Therefore, whenever *R* changes, the process executes, and thus the process updates *Q* with the new value of *R*. *Q* therefore will change whenever *R* changes; in a sense, *Q* has been "wired" to *R*. Note that the process, and hence the concurrent signal assignment, describes a combinational logic process, where the logic is simply a wire.

A concurrent signal assignment statement may include expressions, rather than just one signal, on the right hand side, just as may a signal assignment inside a process.

Figure 4.3 shows a partial testbench for Figure 4.2's multifunction register. That testbench is actually very short; a good testbench would test all the control inputs, and would test different combinations of those inputs too. Note that the testbench initializes all the component inputs and resets the register. The testbench then loads "*1111*", and then shifts right.

The waveforms resulting from simulating the multifunction register with the given testbench are shown in Figure 4.4. The waveforms show the register being cleared to "*0000*", then loaded with "*1111*", and then shifted right on each of the next four clock cycles, resulting in register values of "*0111*", "*0011*", "*0001*", and finally "*0000*".

One might incorrectly assume that another way to update *Q* with the value of *R* would be to instead add the statement "*Q <= R;*" as the last statement in the rising clock *IF* statement in the process of Figure 4.2, just before the second "*END IF;*". However, that approach would not correctly describe the desired behavior. Recall that signals assigned in a process do not actually get updated until after the present simulation cycle completes. Thus, that last statement added to the process would assign *Q* with the *old* value of *R*, and not with the newly-assigned value of *R*. *Q* would thus not be updated until the next time the process executes, which would be on the next rising clock edge, and thus *Q*'s value would always be one cycle behind what the value should be. Alternatively, the concurrent signal assignment "*Q <= R;*" is not sensitive to the clock signal, and instead executes whenever *R* changes (thus executing one delta cycle after *R* is updated).

```
...
   ClkProcess: PROCESS
   ...
   END PROCESS ClkProcess;

   VectorProcess: PROCESS
   BEGIN
      Rst_s <= '1';
      I_s <= "0000";
      Ld_s <= '0'; Shr_s <= '0'; Shl_s <= '0';
      Shr_in_s <= '0'; Shl_in_s <= '0';
      WAIT UNTIL Clk_s='1' AND Clk_s'EVENT;
      WAIT FOR 5 NS;
      Rst_s <= '0';
      I_s <= "1111"; Ld_s <= '1';
      WAIT UNTIL Clk_s='1' AND Clk_s'EVENT;
      WAIT FOR 5 NS;
      Ld_s <= '0'; Shr_s <= '1';
      WAIT UNTIL Clk_s='1' AND Clk_s'EVENT;
      WAIT FOR 5 NS;
      -- Good testbench needs more vectors
      WAIT;
   END PROCESS VectorProcess;
END TBarch;
```

Figure 4.3. Multifunction register testbench.

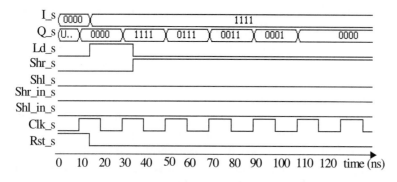

Figure 4.4 Multifunction register waveforms.

4.2 ADDERS

An N-bit adder adds two N-bit binary numbers, resulting in an N-bit binary number representing the sum, and resulting in a carry-out bit. The adder may also include a carry-in bit.

One way to describe an N-bit adder is structurally, as a connection of N full-adders, where each full-adder itself is described either as a connection of gates or perhaps as combinational behavior. Of course, such a structural description represents a carry-ripple implementation of an N-bit adder. Other types of adder implementations, such as a carry-lookahead adder, would require a different structural description.

Another way to describe an N-bit adder is behaviorally. A behavioral description could be created to reflect a carry-ripple implementation or a carry-lookahead implementation, but a nice feature of a behavioral description is its ability to indicate just the functionality of an entity (in this case, the adding of two numbers), without implying a particular implementation (such as carry-ripple or carry-lookahead).

PROCESSES WITH ARITHMETIC OPERATIONS

Given two N-bit inputs A and B, the idea of an implementation-neutral behavioral adder description is to simply describe the adder as computing the sum $A + B$. Figure 4.5 shows such a description. The adder has two 4-bit input ports A and B, and a 4-bit output port S. The architecture consists of a single process, which is sensitive to inputs A and B. Note that if any bit within A or B changes, the process will execute. In particular, not all bits of a vector need to change in order to cause a process to execute; only one bit changing within a vector causes the process to execute.

```
LIBRARY ieee;
USE ieee.std_logic_1164.ALL;
USE ieee.std_logic_unsigned.ALL;

ENTITY Add4 IS
   PORT (A, B: IN std_logic_vector(3 DOWNTO 0);
         S: OUT std_logic_vector(3 DOWNTO 0) );
END Add4;

ARCHITECTURE Beh OF Add4 IS
BEGIN
   PROCESS (A, B)
   BEGIN
      S <= A + B;
   END PROCESS;
END Beh;
```

Figure 4.5 Simple 4-bit adder description.

The process uses the signal assignment statement "$S <= A + B;$". That statement applies the addition operation, "+", to the two *std_logic_vector* ports *A* and *B*. That operation was not defined in the package *ieee.std_logic_1164.ALL*, which instead defined Boolean operations like AND, NAND, OR, NOR, XOR, XNOR, and NOT, for *std_logic* and *std_logic_vector* types. Attempting to compile the description using only the *ieee.std_logic_1164.ALL* package would yield a compiler error stating that "+" is not defined for *std_logic_vector*. Thus, the description uses a second package, *ieee.std_logic_unsigned.ALL*, which defines arithmetic operations "+", "-", "*", and "/" (add, subtract, multiply, and divide), and relational operations "<", "<=", "=", ">=", and ">", for *std_logic_vector* types, assuming the *std_logic_vector* items are unsigned binary numbers. If the items were instead two's complement (signed) numbers, the description would instead use *ieee.std_logic_signed.ALL*, which defines those same arithmetic and relational operations for signed *std_logic_vector* items. An architecture can only use one of those two packages, *ieee.std_logic_signed.ALL* or *ieee.std_logic_unsigned.ALL*, but can not use both. Otherwise, it would not be clear whether operators like "+" should perform signed or unsigned operations.

Figure 4.6 shows a testbench for the simple 4-bit adder of Figure 4.5. The testbench only includes two vectors. A good testbench would instead have many

```
LIBRARY ieee;
USE ieee.std_logic_1164.ALL;

ENTITY Testbench IS
END Testbench;

ARCHITECTURE TBarch OF Testbench IS
   COMPONENT Add4 IS
      PORT (A, B: IN std_logic_vector(3 DOWNTO 0);
            S: OUT std_logic_vector(3 DOWNTO 0) );
   END COMPONENT;

   SIGNAL A_s, B_s, S_s: std_logic_vector(3 DOWNTO 0);

BEGIN
   CompToTest: Add4 PORT MAP (A_s, B_s, S_s);

   PROCESS
   BEGIN
      A_s <= "0011"; B_s <= "0001";
      WAIT FOR 10 ns;
      A_s <= "1100"; B_s <= "0011";
      WAIT FOR 10 ns;
      -- Good testbench needs more vectors
      WAIT;
   END PROCESS;
END TBarch;
```

Figure 4.6 Simple 4-bit adder testbench.

more vectors, would use *ASSERT* statements to check for correct output, and would add blank lines between vectors (all of which are omitted for reasons of brevity here). The testbench illustrates that the testbench file does *not* use the *ieee.std_logic_unsigned.ALL* package, because the testbench does not use arithmetic/relational operators with its *std_logic_vector* types. If instead the testbench used arithmetic/relational operators, such as in an ASSERT statement to check for correct output sums, then the testbench would also have to use that package.

Simulation of the testbench of Figure 4.6 will result in *S_s* first equaling *"0011+0001"*, or *"0100"*. In other words, 3 + 1 equals 4. After 10 ns, *S_s* will equal *"1100+0011"*, or *"1111"*. In other words, 12 + 3 equals 15.

The above example introduced a four-bit adder with no carry-in bit and no carry-out bit. Figure 4.7 illustrates a description having carry-in and carry-out bits, *Ci* and *Co*, respectively. The description uses a technique that extends inputs *A* and *B* into 5-bit numbers, adds them and the carry-in to create a 5-bit sum, and then splits that 5-bit sum into a 1-bit carry-out bit and a 4-bit sum output. The language features involved in that technique will now be discussed.

CONCATENATION

The description in Figure 4.7 uses the concatenation operator. The **concatenation operator**, "&", combines its left and right bit vectors into one larger bit vector value. The description concatenates *'0'* and the four-bit value of *A*, resulting in a

```
LIBRARY ieee;
USE ieee.std_logic_1164.ALL;
USE ieee.std_logic_unsigned.ALL;

ENTITY Add4wCarry IS
   PORT (A, B: IN std_logic_vector(3 DOWNTO 0);
         Ci: IN std_logic;
         S: OUT std_logic_vector(3 DOWNTO 0);
         Co: OUT std_logic );
END Add4wCarry;

ARCHITECTURE Beh OF Add4wCarry IS
BEGIN
   PROCESS (A, B, Ci)
      VARIABLE A5, B5, S5:
         std_logic_vector(4 DOWNTO 0);
   BEGIN
      A5 := '0' & A; B5 := '0' & B;
      S5 := A5 + B5 + Ci;
      S <= S5(3 DOWNTO 0);
      Co <= S5(4);
   END PROCESS;
END Beh;
```

Figure 4.7 4-bit adder description with carry-in and carry-out.

value consisting of the five bits: "$0\ A(3)\ A(2)\ A(1)\ A(0)$". Thus if A were "0011", the result of the concatenation would be "00011".

Concatenation is needed in the description to compute the carry-out bit. If the description had merely computed the sum as "$S <= A + B + Ci;$", the result would have been the correct four-bit sum, but the carry-out bit would not have been computed. Thus, the description first converts the four-bit A and B operands into five-bit operands $A5$ and $B5$ by using the concatenation operator. The description then adds $A5 + B5 + Ci$ into a five-bit value $S5$—the fifth bit of $S5$, namely $S5(4)$, will represent the carry-out bit of the four-bit addition. Finally, the description sets the sum S to the lower four bits of $S5$, namely $S5(3\ DOWNTO\ 0)$, and sets the carry-out bit Co to the fifth bit of $S5$, namely $S5(4)$.

VARIABLES

The description in Figure 4.7 uses a new type of declared object known as a variable. A ***variable declaration*** declares a new storage item and is similar to a signal, except for the important distinction that a variable does not have a time aspect. A variable is defined within a process between the process declaration and the process' begin statement, and can only be accessed within the process in which the variable is defined. (Note: The most modern version of VHDL allows for processes to share variables, but we do not discuss that advanced feature here.) The description first declares a 5-bit *std_logic_vector* variable, named $A5$, using the statement "*VARIABLE A5: std_logic_vector(4 DOWNTO 0);*". Similarly, the description further declares two additional variables $B5$ and $S5$.

The three variables declared within the process are used to calculate the sum and carry-out bits for the 4-bit adder. As previously described, $A5$ and $B5$ are assigned 5-bit versions of the inputs A and B, respectively. Variable assignment uses the operator "$:=$" instead of the signal assignment operator "$<=$". Using the variable assignment operator for assigning a value to a signal, and vice versa, will result in a compilation error.

The language uses different operators primarily for clarity, so that one can immediately distinguish whether an assignment is to a variable or to a signal. Such distinction is important because, unlike signal assignments, variable assignments take effect immediately. The description in Figure 4.7 first assigns the concatenation of '0' and the four-bit input A to the variable $A5$ and assigns the concatenation of '0' and the four-bit input B to the variable $B5$. Because variables (unlike signals) do not have a time aspect, the variables are updated immediately as a process executes, not at the beginning of the next simulation cycle. Thus, the description can immediately use the values assigned to $A5$ and $B5$ to compute the 5-bit sum as "$S5 := A5 + B5 + Ci;$". By defining $S5$ as a variable, the description can access the updated sum value in order to separate it into the final 4-bit sum output, S, and the carry-out output, Co.

Figure 4.8 shows a testbench for the 4-bit adder with carry-in and carry-out of Figure 4.7. The testbench only includes two vectors. As mentioned before, a good

```
LIBRARY ieee;
USE ieee.std_logic_1164.ALL;

ENTITY Testbench IS
END Testbench;

ARCHITECTURE TBarch OF Testbench IS
   COMPONENT Add4wCarry IS
      PORT (A, B: IN std_logic_vector(3 DOWNTO 0);
            Ci: IN std_logic;
            S: OUT std_logic_vector(3 DOWNTO 0);
            Co: OUT std_logic );
   END COMPONENT;

   SIGNAL A_s, B_s, S_s: std_logic_vector(3 DOWNTO 0);
   SIGNAL Ci_s, Co_s: std_logic;

BEGIN
   CompToTest: Add4wCarry
      PORT MAP (A_s, B_s, Ci_s, S_s, Co_s);

   PROCESS
   BEGIN
      A_s <= "0011"; B_s <= "0001"; Ci_s <= '1';
      WAIT FOR 10 ns;
      A_s <= "1100"; B_s <= "0011"; Ci_s <= '0';
      WAIT FOR 10 ns;
      -- Good testbench needs more vectors
      WAIT;
   END PROCESS;
END TBarch;
```

Figure 4.8 Testbench for 4-bit adder with carry-in and carry-out.

testbench would have many more vectors, and would also use *ASSERT* statements to check for correct output. Simulation of the testbench of Figure 4.8 will result in *S_s* first equaling "*0011+0001+1*", or "*0101*". In other words, 3 + 1 + 1 equals 5. After 10 ns, *S_s* will equal "*1100+0011+0*", or "*1111*". In other words, 12 + 3 + 0 equals 15.

4.3 SHIFT REGISTERS

Figure 4.1 presented a multifunction register, which included shift left and shift right operations. If one only requires that the input be serially shifted into the register, a simpler shift register description could be created. Figure 4.9(a) shows a simple 4-bit right shift register, with control input *Shr*, data input *Shr_in*, and parallel 4-bit output *Q*. Figure 4.9(b) shows the register's operations. On every clock

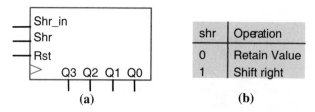

Figure 4.9 4-bit shift register: (a) block diagram, (b) operation table.

cycle that the *Shr* control input is *'1'*, the register shifts the contents one position to the right and loads *Shr_in* into the leftmost bit.

Similar to the multifunction register description of Figure 4.1, the description for the 4-bit shift register in Figure 4.10 declares a signal R as a 4-bit *std_logic_vector*, with that signal being used to store the register contents. The concurrent signal assignment statement *"Q <= R;"* is used to assign the register contents to the output Q. The description performs shifting by assigning the value for each register bit independently as an individual statement, thereby requiring four separate statements to perform the right shift operation. Although such a description is correct, assigning each bit individually results in excessive code for larger registers. For example, a 32-bit shift register would 32 assignment statements. Not only is such code less readable, but such code may contain errors due to cut-and-paste-and-revise errors or due to simply typing the wrong bit number in one of those statements.

Alternatively, the shift operation could be achieved by concatenating each bit of the register together using a single assignment statement: *"R <= Shr_in & R(3) & R(2) & R(1);"*. While simpler and more compact than individual assignment statements, using concatenation is still time-consuming and error prone, as one has to manually enter the bits in the proper order. A loop statement can yield a better description.

PROCESSES WITH FOR LOOP STATEMENTS

Consider a 32-bit version of the shift register of Figure 4.9. Assigning individual bits of the register is very time-consuming. For larger register sizes, a simpler and more compact description utilizes a *loop* to assign the bits. A ***loop statement*** defines a sequence of statements that will be executed repeatedly some number of times. The loop statement contains several items: the loop type, which can be either *FOR* or *WHILE*; the loop parameter, which controls how many times the loop will be executed; and the sequence of statements to be execute during each

```
LIBRARY ieee;
USE ieee.std_logic_1164.ALL;

ENTITY ShiftReg4 IS
    PORT (Q: OUT std_logic_vector(3 DOWNTO 0);
          Shr, Shr_in: IN std_logic;
          Clk, Rst: IN std_logic );
END ShiftReg4;

ARCHITECTURE Beh OF ShiftReg4 IS
    SIGNAL R: std_logic_vector(3 DOWNTO 0);
BEGIN
    PROCESS (Clk)
    BEGIN
        IF (Clk = '1' AND Clk'EVENT) THEN
            IF (Rst = '1') THEN
                R <= "0000";
            ELSIF (Shr = '1') THEN
                R(3) <= Shr_in; R(2) <= R(3);
                R(1) <= R(2); R(0) <= R(1);
            END IF;
        END IF;
    END PROCESS;
    Q <= R;
END Beh;
```

Figure 4.10 4-bit shift register.

loop iteration. The following discussion describes *FOR* loops. *WHILE* loops, will be discussed in a later section.

A ***FOR loop*** is a loop that executes a discrete number of times as specified by the loop parameter. The ***loop parameter*** of a for loop defines the parameter identifier and a range of numbers over which the loop will iterate. For example, the loop declaration "*FOR index IN 0 TO 3 LOOP*" defines a *FOR* loop with a loop parameter identifier named *index* that will iterate from 0 to 3. The *FOR* loop will execute a total of four times, during which *index* will have the values of 0, 1, 2, and 3. The *FOR* loop executes the statement within the body of the loop between the loop declaration and the "*END LOOP;*" statement. Nested loops are allowed, but care must be taken to ensure that all loop parameter identifiers are unique.

Figure 4.11 describes a 32-bit shift register using a *FOR* loop to perform the right shift operation. The shift register includes a reset input, *Rst*, that when '*1*', will reset the contents of the register to all *0*s upon a rising clock edge.

Within the "*IF (Rst = '1') THEN*" statement, the description resets the contents of the register by assigning *R* the hexadecimal value " *X"00000000"* ". A ***hexadecimal number*** describes a number in base 16 format, and is convenient for describing long binary constants. The format involves placing an "*X*" before a vector string. Each character in the subsequent vector string will be considered a hexadecimal digit. Thus, the assignment, "*R <= X"00000000";* " is equivalent to the bitwise assignment "*R <= "00000000000000000000000000000000";* ".

```
LIBRARY ieee;
USE ieee.std_logic_1164.ALL;

ENTITY ShiftReg32 IS
    PORT (Q: OUT std_logic_vector(31 DOWNTO 0);
          Shr, Shr_in: IN std_logic;
          Clk, Rst: IN std_logic );
END ShiftReg32;

ARCHITECTURE Beh OF ShiftReg32 IS
    SIGNAL R: std_logic_vector(31 DOWNTO 0);
BEGIN
    PROCESS (Clk)
    BEGIN
        IF (Clk = '1' AND Clk'EVENT) THEN
            IF (Rst = '1') THEN
                R <= X"00000000";
            ELSIF (Shr = '1') THEN
                R(31) <= Shr_in;
                FOR index IN 0 TO 30 LOOP
                    R(index) <= R(index+1);
                END LOOP;
            END IF;
        END IF;
    END PROCESS;
    Q <= R;
END Beh;
```

Figure 4.11 32-bit shift register description using a FOR loop.

Although the *FOR* loop will execute the loop one iteration at a time, during synthesis the for loop will be expanded, or unrolled, such that all iterations of the loop will be executed simultaneously. For the shift register description, the resulting synthesized circuit would be equivalent to the synthesized hardware circuit had the description specified 32 separate assignments, one for each bit of the shift register.

The description in Figure 4.11 performs the right shift operation by first assigning the input data *Shr_in* to the leftmost bit of the register contents *R*, using the statement "*R(31) <= Shr_in;*". The remaining lower 31 bits of the register will be assigned using a FOR loop. The loop is declared as "*FOR index IN 0 TO 30 LOOP*" and contains a single signal assignment statement, "*R(index) <= R(index+1);*". During each iteration of the loop, the assignment statement within the loop will assign to the bit at the current position, *index*, the value currently stored in the next highest bit location, *index+1*. For example, if *index* were currently equal to 2, the statement "*R(index) <= R(index+1);*" would be equivalent to the statement "*R(2) <= R(3);*", which is how the 4-bit shift register description of Figure 4.10 assigned the individual bits. After executing the loop, all bits of the register contents *R* will have been assigned.

. . .

```
VectorProcess: PROCESS
BEGIN
   Rst_s <= '1';
   Shr_s <= '0'; Shr_in_s <= '0';
   WAIT UNTIL Clk_s='1' AND Clk_s'EVENT;
   WAIT FOR 5 NS;
   Rst_s <= '0';
   WAIT UNTIL Clk_s='1' AND Clk_s'EVENT;
   WAIT FOR 5 NS;
   Shr_s <= '1'; Shr_in_s <= '1';
   FOR index IN 0 TO 15 LOOP
      WAIT UNTIL Clk_s='1' AND Clk_s'EVENT;
   END LOOP;
   WAIT FOR 5 NS;
   ASSERT Q_s = X"FFFF0000"
      REPORT "Failed Q=FFFF0000";
   Shr_s <= '1'; Shr_in_s <= '0';
   FOR index IN 0 TO 15 LOOP
      WAIT UNTIL Clk_s='1' AND Clk_s'EVENT;
   END LOOP;
   WAIT FOR 5 NS;
   ASSERT Q_s = X"0000FFFF"
      REPORT "Failed Q=0000FFFF";
   Shr_s <= '0';
   WAIT;
END PROCESS VectorProcess
```

. . .

Figure 4.12 32-bit shift register testbench.

The description again uses a concurrent signal assignment statement "$Q <= R;$" to assign the register contents to the output Q.

Note that the loop only iterates from 0 to 30, and not over all bits of the register, 0 to 31. This is because the leftmost, or highest-order, bit gets its value from the input *Shr_in*, and thus need not be assigned within the *FOR* loop. If the shift register were instead designed to shift left into the register, the *FOR* loop would instead be declared as "*FOR index IN 1 TO 31 LOOP*", iterating from 1 to 31 and assigning the rightmost, or lowest-order, bit using a separate assignment statement.

A partial testbench for the 32-bit shift register appears in Figure 4.12. The testbench first rests the register contents by setting *Rst_s* to '1', and waits for one clock cycle. Next, the testbench enables the shift operation by setting *Shr_s* to '1', and sets the data input to '1'. The testbench then waits for sixteen clock cycles, which will result in shifting a total of sixteen *1*s into the register. Instead of hard coding sixteen "*WAIT UNTIL Clk_s='1' AND Clk_s'EVENT;*" statements, the testbench also uses a *FOR* loop, which executes sixteen times over the range 0 to 15 and includes only one wait statement. Because the loop parameter identifier itself is not used within the *FOR* loop, that loop could have declared the loop to iterate over any range of size sixteen, such as 100 to 115, or 2 to 17. However, good practice dictates using a range whose purpose clearly indicates sixteen iterations, such as 0 to 15, or perhaps 1 to 16.

After shifting in sixteen *1*s, the testbench verifies the register's output using an *ASSERT* statement to compare *Q_s* with the expected output value of "*X"FFFF0000"* ", reporting "*Failed Q=FFFF0000*" if the assert statement fails.

Using a similar approach, the testbench subsequently shifts in sixteen *0*s and verifies the register output using an *ASSERT* statement to compare the register output with the hexadecimal value "*X"0000FFFF"* ". The testbench then disables the shift control input by setting *Shr_s* to *'0'* and executing the statement "*WAIT;*".

[SIMUL] FILE INPUT/OUTPUT AND SUBPROGRAMS

As designs become more complex and have larger data width for inputs, outputs, and internal signals, specifying a robust set of test vectors with a testbench can become difficult and time-consuming. Thus, as the number of required test vectors increases, designing testbenches using a large sequence of signal assignments, wait statements, and assert statements, may become more difficult. Consider the 32-bit shift register design presented in Figure 4.11 and the corresponding testbench appearing in Figure 4.12. Creating a more robust testbench that shifts into the register several distinct 32-bit values would require hundreds of lines of code. For example, shifting in just one distinct 32-bit test vector requires 64 statements—32 assignment statements assigning the shift data input for each bit, with each assignment followed by a WAIT statement to wait for the next rising clock edge. Defining 100 such vectors would require 64*100 = 6,400 statements.

The approach for testing an entity can be improved by reading the test vectors from an input file. A *file* is a document located on the host computing system, which can be read from or written to within the testbench. Using a file allows for easy inclusion of new test vectors into an existing test vector file, and allows for use of different files that test different design aspects or scenarios. Furthermore, new vectors can be added to the input file without requiring re-compilation in order to re-simulate.

Figure 4.13 shows a testbench that reads test vectors from a file for the 32-bit shift register of Figure 4.11, showing only the testbench vector process. The vector process will read several test vectors from the input file, where the vector file specifies the bits that will be shifted into the register during simulation. The description uses the package *std.textio.ALL,* which defines the *file* type and the supporting subprograms needed to read from a file, specifically *file_open()*, *file_close()*, *endfile()*, *readline()*, and *read()*. A *subprogram* may be either a procedure or a function. A procedure is accessed using a *procedure call*, which is a

```
USE std.textio.ALL;
...
   VectorProcess: PROCESS
      FILE vectorfile: text;
      VARIABLE inputline: line;
      VARIABLE inputbit: bit;
   BEGIN
      file_open(vectorfile, "vectors.txt",
               read_mode);
      Rst_s <= '1';
      Shr_s <= '0'; Shr_in_s <= '0';
      WAIT UNTIL Clk_s='1' AND Clk_s'EVENT;
      WAIT FOR 5 NS;
      Rst_s <= '0';
      WAIT UNTIL Clk_s='1' AND Clk_s'EVENT;
      WAIT FOR 5 NS;
      Shr_s <= '1';
      WHILE NOT endfile(vectorfile) LOOP
         readline(vectorfile, inputline);
         FOR i IN inputline'RANGE LOOP
            read(inputline, inputbit);
            IF inputbit = '1' THEN
               Shr_in_s <= '1';
            ELSE
               Shr_in_s <= '0';
            END IF;
            WAIT UNTIL Clk_s='1' AND Clk_s'EVENT;
         END LOOP;
      END LOOP;
      file_close(vectorfile);
      Shr_s <= '0';
      WAIT;
   END PROCESS VectorProcess;
...
```

Figure 4.13 32-bit shift register testbench with file input.

statement. A function is accessed using a ***function call***, which is an expression and thus returns a value.

The description first declares the file using a file declaration statement. A ***file declaration statement*** defines a file identifier and the file type. The testbench declares the file as "*FILE vectorfile: text;*", which defines a file with the identifier *vectorfile* with a file type of *text*. A ***text file*** is a file that contains an arbitrary number of text (known as "ASCII") characters. The *text* file type is a very convenient file type to use as one can edit a text file with any text editor. The file declaration is specified within the vector process between the PROCESS declaration and the process BEGIN statement, much in the same way as a variable declaration. The testbench also declares two variables, *inputline* and *inputbit*, of types *line* and *bit* respectively, needed for reading the input from the file. The *line* type is defined within *std.textio.ALL* and represents a single line that can be read from or written to a file. The *bit* type is a pre-defined type similar to *std_logic* but can only represent logic values of '0' and '1'

The testbench first opens a file by using the *file_open()* procedure call, before reading or writing to the file. The *file_open()* procedure requires three parameters, a file identifier, the name of the file on the host computing systems, and the file access mode. The **file access mode** can be either *read_mode, write_mode,* or *append_mode* depending on whether the file will be used for input, output, or being appended. The testbench includes the statement "*file_open(vectorfile, "vectors.txt", read_mode);*" that opens the file named "*vectors.txt*" on the host computer system, associates the file with the identifier *vectorfile,* and opens the file for reading.

Before reading from the file, the testbench resets the register contents to *0* by setting the *Rst_s* signal to '1'. The description then sets *Shr_s* to '1' to begin shifting bits into the register. The testbench repeatedly reads bits from *vectorfile* and shift those bits into the register until reaching the end of the file. The testbench uses a WHILE loop. A **WHILE loop** is a loop that continues to execute its statements as long as the loop's condition evaluates to true. The **loop condition** is a Boolean expression that appears between the "*WHILE*" and "*LOOP*" words of a loop declaration, with that condition controlling the execution of the loop. The execution of a WHILE loop is similar to the execution of the previously-presented FOR loop, with the main difference being that the WHILE loop execution is not controlled by a discrete range, but rather by the loop condition. Thus, the number of times a WHILE loop executes may not be known until the loop is actually executed.

The testbench of Figure 4.13 defines a WHILE loop that executes until reaching the end of *vectorfile.* The WHILE loop is declared as "*WHILE NOT endfile(vectorfile) LOOP*", where the loop condition is the Boolean expression "*NOT endfile(vectorfile)*". The *endfile()* function returns *true* if the end of the specified file has been reached, and returns *false* otherwise.

While the end of the *vectorfile* has not been reached, the description uses the *readline()* procedure to read one line at a time from the file. The *readline()* procedure requires two parameters, a *file* parameter and a parameter of type *line.* The procedure call statement "*readline(vectorfile, inputline);*" reads a single line from *vectorfile* and stores the line into the variable *inputline.* The file input and output support within the package *std.textio.ALL* only provides the *readline()* procedure for reading from files, and does not directly support the reading of individual bits. As each line is read from the input file, the testbench needs to use the *read()* procedure to read the individual values from the input line.

The testbench uses a FOR loop to access the individual bits of *inputline.* Recall that a FOR loop's loop parameter must be defined as a discrete range.

Thus, the FOR loop is declared as *"FOR i IN inputline'RANGE LOOP "*, where *"inputline'RANGE"* specifies the number of characters within that line as a discrete range. Within the FOR loop, the testbench reads each bit from *inputline* with the statement *"read(inputline, inputbit);"*. The *read()* procedure takes two parameters, a *line* parameter from which to read and an object into which the procedure will store the value read from the line. The description reads an individual bit from *inputline* and stores the value in the variable *inputbit*, of type *bit*. The *read()* procedure is also defined for other types, including *bit_vector* and *character*, among others.

The testbench can now write the bit read from the input file to the *Shr_in_s* signal. However, the *bit* type and *std_logic* type are not compatible—the direct assignment of a *bit* to a *std_logic*, such as *"Shr_in_s <= inputbit;"*, is not allowed. Instead, the testbench uses an IF statement to assign the value to *Shr_in_s*. If *inputbit* is equal to *'1'*, the IF statement executes the statement *"Shr_in_s <= '1';"*. Otherwise, the testbench executes the ELSE portion of the IF statement, setting *Shr_in_s* to *'0'*. After assigning the shift input data, the testbench will wait until the next rising clock edge before reading the next bit value from the input line, thereby shifting in each bit from the input file into the shift register.

Once the end of the file is reached, the WHILE loop completes and the testbench closes the input file using the *file_close()* procedure. The *file_close()* procedure takes a file identifier as its sole parameter and closes the file, thus disallowing further reading from the file.

Defining the vectors within the *vectors.txt* file allows easy changes to the simulated behavior of the testbench. For example, consider the case when the contents of *vectors.txt* file is:

```
1111111111111111
0000000000000000
```

During simulation, the testbench reads the bits from the file and shifts those bits into the shift register. This input file will first shift sixteen *1*s into the register, followed by sixteen *0*s. The resulting simulation waveform will be identical to the waveform generated from the original testbench that appeared in Figure 4.12.

Figure 4.14 shows the simulation waveform for a 32-bit shift register when the contents of *vectors.txt* are:

```
11
00
```

Notice the four bit values of *'1'*, *'1'*, *'0'*, and *'0'* being shifted into the register.

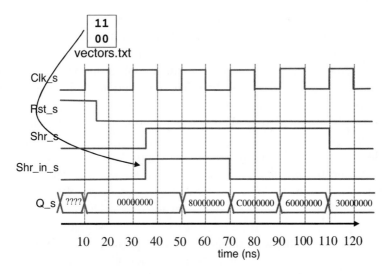

Figure 4.14 32-bit shift register waveform for give vectors.

[SYNTH] COMMON PITFALL

Creating a loop that cannot be unrolled

A common pitfall involves creating an un-synthesizable loop in a description intended for synthesis. In a description intended for synthesis, a loop should be considered merely as a shorthand description for a longer sequence of statements. Consider the FOR loop from Figure 4.11, which is shown again in Figure 4.15 for convenience. That loop is a shorthand description for 31 signal assignment statements: "*R(0) <= R(1);*", "*R(1) <= R(2);*", ..., "*R(30) <= R(31);*". A synthesis tool would in fact "***unroll***" that FOR loop into the equivalent 31 statements that are shown in Figure 4.15. Those statements describe 31 concurrent updates (recall that the order of such statements does not matter) that should occur during a clock cycle of the register that was described in Figure 4.11. The tool is able to unroll the FOR loop because the FOR loop contains clearly indicated bounds of 0 (the lower bound) and 30 (the upper bound). To unroll the loop, the tool simply replicates the loop body 31 times, and for each replicated body instance, the tool

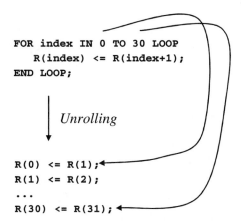

```
FOR index IN 0 TO 30 LOOP
    R(index) <= R(index+1);
END LOOP;
```

Unrolling

```
R(0)  <= R(1);
R(1)  <= R(2);
...
R(30) <= R(31);
```

Figure 4.15 A loop must be un-rollable if the loop is to be synthesized.

replaces the identifier *index* by the value corresponding to that instance (0 for the first instance, 1 for the second instance, etc.).

A common pitfall is to not indicate the bounds of a loop in a manner that a synthesis tool can readily recognize those bounds. If a tool cannot recognize the loop bounds, then the tool does not know how many times to unroll the loop and thus cannot unroll the loop. For example, if the loop were described as "*FOR index IN 0 TO Regwidth LOOP* ", and *Regwidth* were declared as anything other than a constant (e.g., as a signal, port, or variable), then a synthesis tool might not be able to determine the value of *Regwidth* and thus might not be able to unroll the loop. If an RTL synthesis tool cannot unroll a loop, the tool cannot synthesize the loop.

WHILE loops are also generally not synthesizable, because synthesis tools generally are not able to unroll such loops due to not recognizing the loop bounds. Some synthesis tools are actually able to unroll certain types of WHILE loops that are essentially equivalent to FOR loops, such as the following example of a WHILE loop:

```
index := 0;
WHILE (index < 31) LOOP
    ... -- loop statements
    index := index + 1;
END LOOP;
```

Assuming that *index* is declared as an integer variable, a tool might recognize that the WHILE loop is equivalent to the above mentioned FOR loop, and thus a tool might unroll the loop. However, because many synthesis tools will not recognize the WHILE loop as unrollable, it is best to only use FOR loops with explicit bounds in descriptions intended for synthesis.

Figure 4.12 and Figure 4.13 also used loops. However, whether or not those loops can be unrolled is not relevant, because those loops appear in a testbench, which will not be synthesized.

4.4 COMPARATORS

An N-bit comparator compares two N-bit numbers A and B and indicates whether A is greater than, less than, or equal to B. Creating a behavioral description for either two unsigned numbers, or for two signed numbers, should be straightforward based on earlier discussions. However, creating a behavioral description of a special comparator (used mainly for demonstration purposes here) that compares an unsigned number A with a signed number B is not obvious, and thus will be discussed in this section.

Section 4.2 presented a behavioral description of a 4-bit adder in which the 4-bit *std_logic_vector* inputs and outputs were treated as unsigned values by using the package *ieee.std_logic_unsigned.ALL*. That section also mentioned that using *ieee.std_logic_signed.ALL* would have treated *std_logic_vector* as signed numbers. However, those packages do not allow the use of both unsigned and signed numbers within the same architecture.

Sometimes such simultaneous use of unsigned and signed logic vectors is indeed required within a single architecture, as would be the case for a 4-bit magnitude comparator that compares an unsigned 4-bit number A with a signed 4-bit number B. A block diagram of that comparator appears in Figure 4.16(a).

UNSIGNED AND SIGNED NUMBERS

A solution to using both signed and unsigned logic vectors in the same architecture is to use the package *ieee.std_logic_arith.ALL*, which includes two logic vector types named *signed* and *unsigned*, and also defines operators +, -, *, /, <, <=, =, >=, and > for any combination of unsigned and signed operands. For example, the package defines the + operator for adding two unsigned numbers, two signed numbers, or an unsigned and signed number (in either order).

Figure 4.16(b) illustrates use of those types to describe the special comparator introduced above. The description declares port A as type *unsigned*, and declared port B as type *signed*. The description then uses the comparison "$A < B$", which will correctly compare the unsigned and signed items. Although the description does not do so, objects of *unsigned* or *signed* type may have individual bits accessed just like for *std_logic_vector*, e.g., $A(2)$ corresponds to the value of bit 2

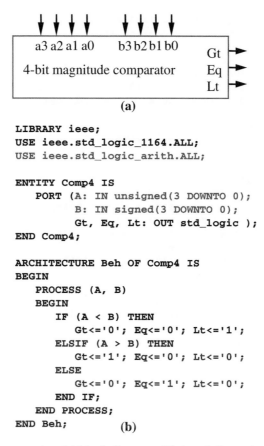

(a)

```
LIBRARY ieee;
USE ieee.std_logic_1164.ALL;
USE ieee.std_logic_arith.ALL;

ENTITY Comp4 IS
    PORT (A: IN unsigned(3 DOWNTO 0);
          B: IN signed(3 DOWNTO 0);
          Gt, Eq, Lt: OUT std_logic );
END Comp4;

ARCHITECTURE Beh OF Comp4 IS
BEGIN
    PROCESS (A, B)
    BEGIN
      IF (A < B) THEN
          Gt<='0'; Eq<='0'; Lt<='1';
      ELSIF (A > B) THEN
          Gt<='1'; Eq<='0'; Lt<='0';
      ELSE
          Gt<='0'; Eq<='1'; Lt<='0';
      END IF;
    END PROCESS;
END Beh;
```
                              (b)

Figure 4.16 4-bit comparator: (a) block diagram, (b) description using both unsigned and signed types in one architecture.

in the 4-bit unsigned vector *A*. The remainder of the description in Figure 4.16 is straightforward.

Figure 4.17 shows a testbench for the comparator. The testbench also uses the package *ieee.std_logic_arith.ALL* so that the component port types of *unsigned* and *signed* are recognized, and so that signals of those types can be declared for use by the vector process. The testbench includes vectors that test both positive and negative values of *B*, and includes vectors in which *A* is greater than, less than, and equal to *B*.

One may wonder why one would ever use the earlier-introduce packages *ieee.std_logic_unsigned* and *ieee.std_logic_signed* when the package *ieee.std_logic_arith* handles both unsigned and signed numbers. The drawback of using *ieee.std_logic_arith* is that its types *signed* and *unsigned* are not compatible with the widely-used type *std_logic_vector*.

```
LIBRARY ieee;
USE ieee.std_logic_1164.ALL;
USE ieee.std_logic_arith.ALL;
...

    SIGNAL A_s: unsigned(3 DOWNTO 0);
    SIGNAL B_s: signed(3 DOWNTO 0);
    SIGNAL Gt_s, Eq_s, Lt_s: std_logic;

BEGIN
    CompToTest: Comp4 PORT MAP (A_s, B_s,
       Gt_s, Eq_s, Lt_s);

    PROCESS
    BEGIN
       A_s <= "0011"; B_s <= "0001";
       WAIT FOR 10 ns;
       A_s <= "1111"; B_s <= "0111";
       WAIT FOR 10 ns;
       A_s <= "0111"; B_s <= "1011";
       WAIT FOR 10 ns;
       A_s <= "0001"; B_s <= "0010";
       WAIT FOR 10 ns;
       A_s <= "0001"; B_s <= "0001";
       WAIT FOR 10 ns;
       A_s <= "0000"; B_s <= "1111";
       WAIT FOR 10 ns;
       WAIT;
    END PROCESS;
END TBarch;
```

Figure 4.17 4-bit comparator testbench.

Although packages *ieee.std_logic_unsigned*, *ieee.std_logic_signed*, and *ieee.std_logic_arith* all have "*ieee*" at the beginning of their names, they are not actually IEEE standards. They were instead developed by a particular company (Synopsys), and made available for public use. As such, specific implementations of those packages by different companies could have variations. An IEEE standard does exist to deal with signed and unsigned numbers, embodied in the packages *ieee.numeric_bit* and *ieee.numeric_std*, but tool support for those packages, at the time of this book's writing, is not widespread. Future evolution of the packages and tools may result in changes to handling of signed and unsigned numbers.

4.5 REGISTER FILES

A register file can provide for compact storage when a design contains multiple registers. Register files come in different sizes. A 4x32 register file has 4 registers, each being 32 bits wide. Figure 4.18(a) shows a structural design of a 4x32 regis-

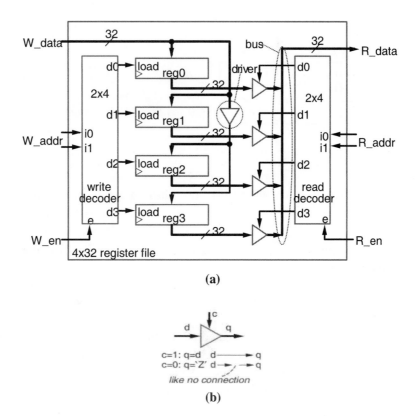

(a)

c=1: q=d   d————►q
c=0: q='Z' d—►, —►q
like no connection

(b)

Figure 4.18 Register file: (a) 4x32 register file, (b) functionality of three-state buffers, used to enable wiring together of register outputs.

ter file having what is known as one "write port" and one "read port" (not to be confused with VHDL ports).

The register file design uses two 2x4 decoders with enable. Chapter 2 provided the description of a 2x4 decoder. Adding an enable input, which when '0' causes all decoder outputs to be '0', would be a simple extension of that description.

The register file design also uses three-state buffers (each buffer shown in the figure actually corresponds to 32 buffers), whose functionality is illustrated in Figure 4.18(b). When the control input is '1', the buffer passes its data input to its output. However, when the control input is '0', the buffer outputs a special value known as "high impedance" and written as 'Z'. A wire with a high impedance value essentially appears to be disconnected from other wires to which it is actually connected. The purpose of the three-state buffers is to allow the register outputs to simply be wired together to form a bus, rather than being fed through a large and slow multiplexor before reaching the read port's data output. Such bus wiring works correctly only if the design is such that no more than one register

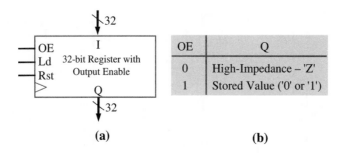

(a)   **(b)**

Figure 4.19 Register with output enable: (a) block diagram, (b) output enable functionality.

can ever output non-high-impedance values onto the bus. The decoder ensures such behavior.

The register file design in Figure 4.18 also contains a signal-strengthening driver, but we can omit that from a register file description, as such drivers would automatically be inserted by a synthesis tool.

The three-state buffers can be treated as internal parts of the registers. Thus, the register file design would require the design of a 32-bit register component having a load control input and an output enable control input (and having internal three-state buffers). The block diagram and functionality of such a register is shown in Figure 4.19.

HIGH-IMPEDANCE VALUES IN STD_LOGIC AND STD_LOGIC_VECTOR

Figure 4.20 provides a description of a register with output enable. The description will make use of the fact that the *std_logic* and *std_logic_vector* types directly support high-impedance values. Objects of those types can be set to '*Z*' just as they could be set to '*0*' or '*1*'. For example, a signal *S* of type *std_logic* could be assigned a high-impedance value simply by using the statement "*S* <= 'Z';". Thus, the description need not introduce a new logic type, and instead uses *std_logic_vector* for its register output *Q*.

The description uses two processes. *RegProcess* describes the main storage and reset behavior of the register, as in previous register descriptions. Note that the process includes the statement "*R* <= (*OTHERS*=>'0');". That statement assigns *0*s to all 32 bits of the vector *R*, essentially having the same behavior as the assignment statement "*R* <= X"00000000";", but happens to do so using a new notation involving "*OTHERS*". The notation is a bit awkward due to actually being usable in a more general scenario, but the notation is commonly used to set

```
LIBRARY ieee;
USE ieee.std_logic_1164.ALL;

ENTITY Reg32wOE IS
   PORT (I: IN std_logic_vector(31 DOWNTO 0);
         Q: OUT std_logic_vector(31 DOWNTO 0);
         Oe, Ld: IN std_logic;
         Clk, Rst: IN std_logic );
END Reg32wOE;

ARCHITECTURE Beh OF Reg32wOE IS
   SIGNAL R: std_logic_vector(31 DOWNTO 0);
BEGIN
   RegProcess: PROCESS (Clk)
   BEGIN
      IF (Clk = '1' AND Clk'EVENT) THEN
         IF (Rst = '1') THEN
            R <= (OTHERS=>'0');
         ELSIF (Ld = '1') THEN
            R <= I;
         END IF;
      END IF;
   END PROCESS;

   OutputProcess: PROCESS (R, Oe)
   BEGIN
      IF (Oe = '1') THEN
         Q <= R;
      ELSE
         Q <= (OTHERS=>'Z');
      END IF;
   END PROCESS;
END Beh;
```

Figure 4.20 Description of register with output enable.

all bits of a vector to a particular value as used here. This notation is not only somewhat shorter, but is also independent of the number of bits in the vector.

OutputProcess describes the combinational logic of the three-state buffer output behavior of the register. When the output enable input is *'1'*, the process sets the output *Q* to the stored value *R*. When the output enable input is *'0'*, the process sets the output *Q* to high impedance, or to all *Z*s. The process also happens to use the new vector assignment notation involving "*OTHERS*", namely "*Q <= (OTHERS=>'Z');*". Here, the advantage of the others notation becomes quite evident, as the alternative assignment statement would have been "*Q <= "ZZZZZZZZZZZZZZZZZZZZZZZZZZZZZZZZ";*", because that statement could not have used the hexadecimal notation to reduce the size of the right side of the statement.

```
...
   VectorProcess: PROCESS
   BEGIN
      Rst_s <= '1';
      Oe_s <= '1'; Ld_s <= '0';
      I_s <= X"00000000";
      WAIT UNTIL Clk_s='1' AND Clk_s'EVENT;
      WAIT FOR 5 NS;
      Rst_s <= '0';
      WAIT UNTIL Clk_s='1' AND Clk_s'EVENT;
      WAIT FOR 5 NS;
      Ld_s <= '1'; I_s <= X"000000FF";
      WAIT UNTIL Clk_s='1' AND Clk_s'EVENT;
      WAIT FOR 5 NS;
      ASSERT Q_s = X"000000FF"
         REPORT "Failed output enabled";
      Ld_s <= '0'; Oe_s <= '0';
      WAIT FOR 5 NS;
      ASSERT
         Q_s = "ZZZZZZZZZZZZZZZZZZZZZZZZZZZZZZZZ"
         REPORT "Failed output disabled";
      WAIT;
   END PROCESS VectorProcess;
...
```

Figure 4.21 Partial testbench for register with output enable.

A partial testbench for a register with output enable appears in Figure 4.21. The vector process enables the register output, performs a load, and checks to see that the loaded data appears at the register's output. The process then disables the register output, and checks that the output value becomes high impedance.

Note that the "*OTHERS*" notation cannot be used in the assert statement's condition. The "*OTHERS*" notation only applies to an assignment statement, and cannot be used within a condition. Instead, the assert condition must compare with a 32-bit string of *Z*s.

Given this description of a register with output enable, the register file structural design of Figure 4.18 could be described using the earlier-discussed structural description method of instantiating and connecting components. In this case, the description would instantiate two decoders with enable and four registers with output enable, and would connect those components together and with external inputs and outputs as shown in Figure 4.18. Such a structural description appears in Figure 4.22.

```
LIBRARY ieee;
USE ieee.std_logic_1164.ALL;

ENTITY RegFile4x32 IS
    PORT (R_Addr, W_Addr: IN std_logic_vector(3 DOWNTO 0);
            R_en, W_en: IN std_logic;
            R_Data: OUT std_logic_vector(31 DOWNTO 0);
            W_Data: IN std_logic_vector(31 DOWNTO 0);
            Clk, Rst: IN std_logic );
END RegFile4x32;

ARCHITECTURE Struct OF RegFile4x32 IS
    COMPONENT Dcd2x4wEn IS
        PORT (i1, i0, en: IN std_logic;
                d3, d2, d1, d0: OUT std_logic);
    END COMPONENT;
    COMPONENT Reg32wOE IS
        PORT (I: IN std_logic_vector(31 DOWNTO 0);
                Q: OUT std_logic_vector(31 DOWNTO 0);
                Oe, Ld: IN std_logic;
                Clk, Rst: IN std_logic );
    END COMPONENT;
    SIGNAL W_d3, W_d2, W_d1, W_d0: std_logic;
    SIGNAL R_d3, R_d2, R_d1, R_d0: std_logic;
BEGIN
    R_Dcd: Dcd2x4wEn PORT MAP(R_Addr(1),R_Addr(0),R_en,
                        R_d3,R_d2,R_d1,R_d0);
    W_Dcd: Dcd2x4wEn PORT MAP(W_Addr(1),W_Addr(0),W_en,
                        W_d3,W_d2,W_d1,W_d0);
    Reg0: Reg32wOE PORT MAP(W_Data,R_Data,R_d0,W_d0,Clk,Rst);
    Reg1: Reg32wOE PORT MAP(W_Data,R_Data,R_d1,W_d1,Clk,Rst);
    Reg2: Reg32wOE PORT MAP(W_Data,R_Data,R_d2,W_d2,Clk,Rst);
    Reg3: Reg32wOE PORT MAP(W_Data,R_Data,R_d3,W_d3,Clk,Rst);
END Struct;
```

Figure 4.22 Structural description of a 4x32 register file.

[SIMUL] DRIVERS AND RESOLUTION FUNCTIONS

The previous section created a description in which certain signals had multiple drivers. A ***driver*** is the name for the object that keeps track of the values that a process writes to a signal. If a process contains a signal assignment statement for a signal, the process will have a driver for that signal. In earlier sections, each signal had only a single driver, i.e., only one process wrote to any particular signal. In the previous section, however, the signal *R_Data* has four drivers—one from *Reg0*'s *OutputProcess* (which writes to output port *Q*, which in turn is mapped to signal *R_Data*), one from *Reg1*'s *OutputProcess*, one from *Reg2*'s *OutputProcess*, and one from *Reg3*'s *OutputProcess*. Note that each instantiation of the *Reg32wOE* component results in a unique instance of *OutputProcess*, ultimately resulting in four processes that each drive *R_Data*. Albeit, care was taken to ensure that only one such process at a time could drive a value of '*0*' or '*1*', with the other processes driving '*Z*'. Nevertheless, the signal at any time will have four values being written to it, three of which will be *Z*s, and the fourth of which might be '*0*', '*1*', or '*Z*'. The simulator must have a method for resolving these multiple driving values of a signal into a single value for the signal. A resolution function represents such a method. A ***resolution function*** is a function that takes multiple values for a signal, and returns a single value. If a signal will have multiple drivers, then its subtype must have an associated resolution function, otherwise an error occurs. When faced with multiple driving values of a signal, the simulator automatically calls the signal subtype's associated resolution function to resolve the multiple values into one value.

Recall that the *R_Data* signal is declared as subtype *std_logic_vector*. That subtype is declared in the *ieee.std_logic_1164.ALL* package. That subtype declaration, which we have not shown, includes a resolution function. That resolution function returns '*1*' if one of the drivers is '*1*' and the others are all '*Z*'. It returns '*0*' if one of the drivers is '*0*' and the others are all '*Z*'. It returns '*Z*' if all the drivers are '*Z*'. However, if two (or more) of the drivers are '*0*' or '*1*', then the resolution function returns the value '*X*'. '*X*' is another possible *std_logic* value, meaning "unknown".

Creation of resolution functions is an advanced topic, further coverage of which is beyond the scope of this book.

ARRAYS

As was the case for several other components, the register file can be described behaviorally rather than structurally. A behavioral description appears in Figure 4.23. The description declares a new type, called *regfile_type*, as an array. An ***array*** is another form of type declaration that describes an object consisting of a number of elements, all having the same subtype, and each being accessible using an index. The description declares *regfile_type* as consisting of elements whose indices are numbered from 0 to 3 (meaning 0, 1, 2, and 3), thus comprising four elements in total, and whose subtypes are all 32-bit *std_logic_vector*. The description then declares one signal *regfile* of type *regfile_type*. An array element is accessed using an index. For example, the reset portion of the description sets the first array element to *0*s using the statement "*regfile(0) <= X"00000000";*". In that statement, the index is *0*. The description then sets the second, third, and fourth elements using similar statements, having indices of 1, 2, and 3.

The description consists of two processes. *WriteProcess* handles writes to the register. During a normal write, the *regfile* array index is not a constant as above, but is instead the value of the input port *W_addr*, which is a 4-bit vector. Unfortunately, one cannot use a vector as an array index; the index must be a numeric type

```
LIBRARY ieee;
USE ieee.std_logic_1164.ALL;
USE ieee.std_logic_unsigned.ALL;
...
ARCHITECTURE Beh OF RegFile4x32 IS
    TYPE regfile_type IS
        ARRAY (0 TO 3) OF std_logic_vector(31 DOWNTO 0);
    SIGNAL regfile : regfile_type;
BEGIN
    WriteProcess: PROCESS(Clk)
    BEGIN
        IF (Clk = '1' AND Clk'EVENT) THEN
            IF (Rst = '1') THEN
                regfile(0) <= X"00000000";
                regfile(1) <= X"00000000";
                regfile(2) <= X"00000000";
                regfile(3) <= X"00000000";
            ELSIF (W_en = '1') THEN
                regfile(conv_integer(W_Addr)) <= W_Data;
            END IF;
        END IF;
    END PROCESS;

    ReadProcess: PROCESS(R_Addr, R_en, regfile)
    BEGIN
        IF (R_en = '1') THEN
            R_Data <= regfile(conv_integer(R_Addr));
        ELSE
            R_Data <= (OTHERS=>'Z');
        END IF;
    END PROCESS;
END Beh;
```

Figure 4.23 Behavioral description of a 4x32 register file.

(such as an integer). Thus, the statement *"regfile(W_addr) <= W_data;"* is not allowed. To cope with this limitation, the package *ieee.std_logic_unsigned.ALL* includes a function named *Conv_Integer. Conv_Integer* takes a *std_logic_vector* as a parameter, and returns an integer. Similar functions with the same name exist in the *ieee.std_logic_signed.ALL* and *ieee.std_logic_arith.ALL* packages. Thus, *Conv_Integer* is commonly used to convert a vector into an integer when indexing an array. Most synthesis tools support the *Conv_Integer* function.

CHAPTER 5

Register-Transfer Level (RTL) Design

5.1 HIGH-LEVEL STATE MACHINE (HLSM) BEHAVIOR

Register-transfer level (RTL) design involves describing the behavior of a design as the transfers that occur between registers every clock cycle. One method for such description uses a high-level state machine (HLSM) computation model. The finite-state machine (FSM) model of Chapter 3 allows only Boolean operations and conditions in states and transitions. In contrast, the HLSM model allows arithmetic operations and conditions, such as the addition or comparison of two 8-bit binary numbers. Furthermore, the HLSM model allows explicit declaration of registers, which may be written to and read from in the HLSM's states and transitions.

Figure 5.1 shows an FSM and an HLSM model for the three-cycles-high laser timer system of Section 3.2, whose behavior is such that when a button press is detected, the system holds an output high for exactly three clock cycles. Figure 5.1(a) shows an FSM description of the system, which uses three states to hold the output high for three cycles. However, what if the system was supposed to hold its output high for 512 cycles rather than just three cycles? Creating an FSM with 512 states to hold the output high would result in an unnecessarily large description. For such a system, a high-level state machine model would be more appropriate. Figure 5.1(b) shows a description having identical behavior with the FSM description of Figure 5.1(a) but achieved using a high-level state machine model. The HLSM has only two states, and explicitly declares a 2-bit register *cnt*. The register *cnt* is used to count the number of cycles for which the output has been

Inputs: b; Outputs: x

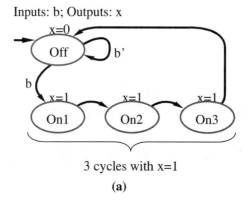

3 cycles with x=1

(a)

Inputs: b; Outputs: x; Register: cnt(2)

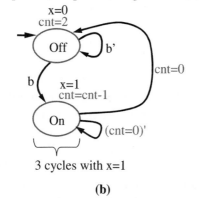

3 cycles with x=1

(b)

Figure 5.1 Two state machine description types: (a) FSM, (b) high-level state machine (HLSM).

held high. The first state initializes *cnt* to 2. After a button press has been detected, the second state holds the output high while comparing *cnt* to *0* and also decrementing *cnt*. The net result is that the output will be held high for three clock cycles. Initializing *cnt* to 511 (and also declaring *cnt* to be a 9-bit register rather than just 2-bits) would result in holding the output high for 512 cycles.

Describing an HLSM in VHDL can be achieved using a straightforward approach similar to the approach for describing an FSM. Similar to the approach for an FSM, the approach for an HLSM considers the target architecture consisting of a combinational logic part and a register part, as shown in Figure 5.2. The earlier-introduced FSM register part consisted only of a state register. The HLSM register part consists of a state register, and of any explicitly declared registers. The figure shows the architecture for the laser timer example system, which has one explicitly declared register, *cnt*.

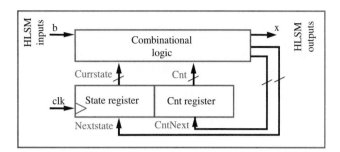

Figure 5.2 Target architecture for an HLSM, consisting of a combinational logic part, and a register part.

Describing an HLSM in VHDL follows straightforwardly from the target architecture, as illustrated in Figure 5.3. The description consists of two processes, one for the combinational logic, and one for the registers. In addition to declaring current and next signals for the state register as for an FSM, the description also declares current and next signals for each explicitly declared register in the HLSM. For the laser timer example's one explicit register *cnt*, the description declares two signals, *Cnt* and *CntNext*. In order to support arithmetic operations and conditions involving that register, the description also uses the library *ieee.std_logic_unsigned.ALL*.

```
LIBRARY ieee;
USE ieee.std_logic_1164.ALL;
USE ieee.std_logic_unsigned.ALL;

ENTITY LaserTimer IS
    PORT (b: IN std_logic;
          x: OUT std_logic;
          Clk, Rst: IN std_logic );
END LaserTimer;

ARCHITECTURE HLSM OF LaserTimer IS
    TYPE Statetype IS (S_Off, S_On);
    SIGNAL Currstate, Nextstate: Statetype;
    SIGNAL Cnt, CntNext: std_logic_vector(1 DOWNTO 0);
BEGIN
    CombLogic: PROCESS (Currstate, Cnt, b)
    BEGIN

       ...
    END PROCESS CombLogic;

    Regs: PROCESS (Clk)
    BEGIN

       ...
    END PROCESS Regs;

END HLSM;
```

Figure 5.3 Code template for describing the laser timer's HLSM in VHDL.

```
  ...
ARCHITECTURE HLSM OF LaserTimer IS
   TYPE Statetype IS (S_Off, S_On);
   SIGNAL Currstate, Nextstate: Statetype;
   SIGNAL Cnt, CntNext: std_logic_vector(1 DOWNTO 0);
BEGIN
   CombLogic: PROCESS (Currstate, Cnt, b)
   BEGIN
      CASE Currstate IS
         WHEN S_Off =>                      Note: Writes
            x <= '0';                       are to "next"
            CntNext <= "10";                signal, reads
            IF (b = '0') THEN               are from
               Nextstate <= S_Off;          "current"
            ELSE                            signal. See
               Nextstate <= S_On;           target
            END IF;                        architecture to
         WHEN S_On =>                       understand
            x <= '1';                       why.
            CntNext <= Cnt - "01";
            IF (Cnt = "00") THEN
               Nextstate <= S_Off;
            ELSE
               Nextstate <= S_On;
            END IF;
      END CASE;
   END PROCESS CombLogic; ...
```

Figure 5.4 HLSM combinational part.

Figure 5.4 shows the process for the combinational logic part of the HLSM. The process is sensitive to all the inputs to the combinational logic. Figure 5.2 shows those inputs to be the signals coming from the registers, namely *Currstate* and *Cnt*, and the external input *b*. The process consists of a case statement that executes the actions and transitions associated with the current state. Figure 5.1(b) shows those actions to be not just the setting of the HLSM's external outputs (e.g., "*x=0*"), but also setting of explicitly declared registers (e.g., "*cnt=2*"). The actions in the process of Figure 5.4 therefore includes not only setting of the external output values (e.g., "*x <= '0';*"), but also setting of the next values for explicitly defined registers (e.g., "*CntNext <= "10";*").

Note from the architecture shown in Figure 5.2 that for an explicitly declared register, the combinational logic reads the current signal (*Cnt*) but writes the next signal (*CntNext*) for the *cnt* register. This dichotomy explains why the action "*cnt <= cnt - 1*" of the HLSM in Figure 5.1(b) is described in the process of Figure 5.4 as "*CntNext <= Cnt - "01";*". Reading is from *Cnt*, while writing is to *CntNext*. When describing HLSMs in an HDL, care must be taken to ensure that reads are from current signals and writes are to next signals for explicitly declared registers.

```
...
ARCHITECTURE HLSM OF LaserTimer IS
   TYPE Statetype IS (S_Off, S_On);
   SIGNAL Currstate, Nextstate: Statetype;
   SIGNAL Cnt, CntNext: std_logic_vector(1 DOWNTO 0);
BEGIN
   CombLogic: PROCESS (Currstate, Cnt, b)
   ...
   END PROCESS CombLogic;

   Regs: PROCESS (Clk)
   BEGIN
      IF (Clk = '1' AND Clk'EVENT) THEN
         IF (Rst = '1') THEN
            Currstate <= S_Off;
            Cnt <= "00";
         ELSE
            Currstate <= Nextstate;
            Cnt <= CntNext;
         END IF;
      END IF;
   END PROCESS Regs;

END HLSM;
```

Figure 5.5 HLSM register part.

The transitions in the process in Figure 5.4, when reading from an explicitly declared register, must read from the current signal and not the next signal, again based on the target architecture of Figure 5.2. Thus, the transition that detects *cnt=0* appears as "*Cnt = "00";*".

Figure 5.5 shows the process for the register part of the HLSM. The register part actually describes two registers—the state register (involving signals *Currstate* and *Nextstate*), and the *cnt* register (involving signals *Cnt* and *CntNext*). When the clock is rising and reset is not asserted, the process updates each current signal with the corresponding next signal. If instead reset was asserted, the process sets each current signal to an initial value. Note that the process resets *Cnt* to an initial value ("*00*"), even though such reset behavior is not strictly necessary for correct functioning of the HLSM. Such reset behavior was included to follow the modeling guidelines described in Chapter 3, where it was stated that all registers should have defined reset behavior.

Figure 5.6 provides simulation waveforms generated when using the laser timer example testbench introduced in Chapter 3. Note first that the three-cycle-high behavior is identical to the FSM behavior from Chapter 3. The waveforms show two internal signals, *Cnt* and *Currstate*. Note how the system enters state *S_On* on the first rising clock after *b* becomes '*1*', causing *Cnt* to be initialized to

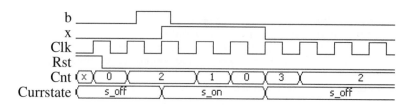

Figure 5.6 HLSM simulation results.

2. Cnt is then decremented on each rising clock while in state *S_On*. After *Cnt* reaches *0, Currstate* changes to *S_Off*. Note that *Cnt* also was decremented at that time, causing *Cnt* to wrap around from *0* to *3* ("*00*" - '*1*' = "*11*"), but that value of *3* was never used, because state *S_Off* sets *Cnt* to *2* again.

Examining the reset behavior of the system is useful. At the beginning of simulation, *Cnt* is undefined. At the first rising clock, *Cnt* is reset to *0* by the description's explicit reset behavior. At the next rising clock, *Cnt* is set to *2* by state *S_Off*. Also note that *Currstate* starts with the value *S_Off*. Actually, *Currstate* should have also been undefined until the first rising clock, but the commercial simulator used to generate the above waveforms happened to give *Currstate* the initial value of *S_Off*. Care must be taken never to rely on such simulator-specific initialization, and instead to always explicitly initialize all registers as part of a system's reset behavior.

5.2 TOP-DOWN DESIGN— HLSM TO CONTROLLER AND DATAPATH

Recall from Chapters 2 and 3 that top-down design involves first capturing and simulating the behavior of a system, and then transforming that behavior to structure and simulating again. Top-down design divides the design problem into two steps. The first step is to get the behavior right (freed from the complexity of designing structure), and the second step is to derive a structural implementation for that behavior. Dividing into two steps can make the design process proceed more smoothly than trying to directly capture structure. The two-step approach also enables the use of automated tools that automatically convert the behavior to structure.

At the register-transfer level, top-down design involves converting a high-level state machine (HLSM) to a structural design consisting of a controller and a datapath, as shown in Figure 5.7. The datapath carries out the arithmetic operations involved in the HLSM's actions and conditions. The controller sequences

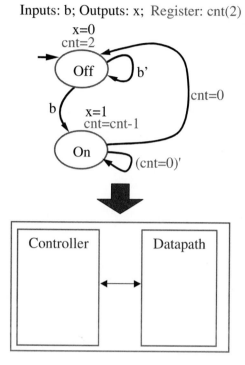

Inputs: b; Outputs: x; Register: cnt(2)

Figure 5.7 Top-down design at the RT level involves converting an HLSM to a controller and datapath implementation.

those operations in the datapath. The controller itself will be an implementation of an FSM.

The first step in converting an HLSM to a controller and datapath is typically to design a datapath that is capable of implementing all the arithmetic operations of the HLSM. Figure 5.8 shows a datapath capable of implementing the arithmetic operations of the laser timer HLSM.

The datapath includes a register *Cnt*, a decrementer to compute *Cnt-1*, and a comparator to detect when *Cnt* is *0*. Those components are connected to enable the operations needed by the HLSM, with a mux in front of the *Cnt* register to account for the fact that *Cnt* can be loaded from two different sources. The datapath provides clear names for the input and output control signals of the datapath (*Cnt_s*, *Cnt_eq0*, and *Cnt_ld*).

Inputs: b; Outputs: x; Register: cnt(2)

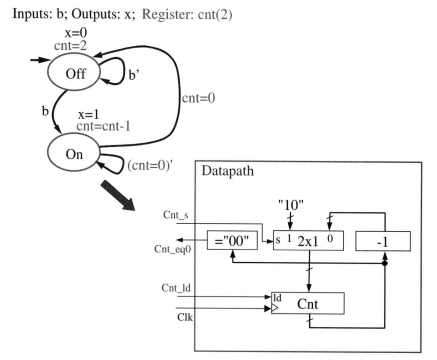

Figure 5.8 Deriving a datapath for the arithmetic operations for the laser timer HLSM.

After creating a datapath, the next step is to derive a controller by replacing the HLSM with an FSM having the same state and transition structure, but replacing arithmetic operations by Boolean operations that use the datapath input and output control signals to carry out the desired arithmetic operations inside the datapath. Such an FSM is shown in Figure 5.9. The FSM does not contain an explicit register declaration for *cnt*, as that register now appears in the datapath. Likewise, any writes of that register have been replaced by writes to datapath control signals that configure the input to the register and enable a register load. For example, the assignment "*cnt* = 2" in state *Off* has been replaced by the Boolean actions "*Cnt_s=1*", which configures the datapath mux to pass "*10*" (2) through the mux, and "*Cnt_ld=1*", which enables loading of the *Cnt* register.

Proceeding with top-down design requires describing Figure 5.9's controller and datapath in VHDL. One option would be to create an entity for the controller and an entity for the datapath, and then instantiating and connecting a controller and datapath component in another higher-level entity. However, a simpler approach describes the controller and datapath as processes within a single architecture. The simpler approach will now be discussed.

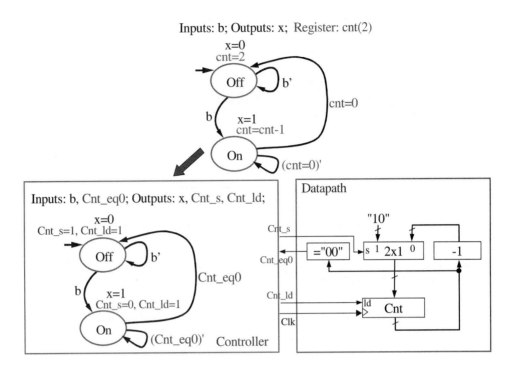

Figure 5.9 Deriving a controller by replacing the HLSM with an FSM that uses the datapath to carry out arithmetic operations.

The datapath could be described structurally. Such a description would instantiate four components: a register, a comparator, a mux, and a decrementer. The description would connect those four components. Each component would require further description as its own entity.

The datapath could instead be described behaviorally. Recall from Chapters 2 and 3 that behavioral descriptions are typically easier to create and to understand than structural descriptions. Of course, a behavioral description would need to be further converted to structure to achieve an implementation, meaning that top-down design must be applied in a hierarchical manner.

One approach to behaviorally describing the datapath involves partitioning the datapath into a combinational logic part and a register part, as shown in Figure 5.10. Notice the similarity of this architecture with the architecture in Figure 5.2, which also consists of a combinational logic part and a register part.

Describing the datapath architecture in VHDL thus proceeds in the same manner as in that previous situation, namely using two processes, one for any combi-

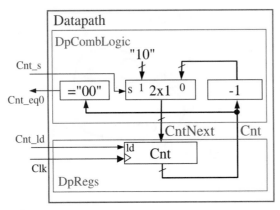

Figure 5.10 Partitioning a datapath into a combinational logic part, and a register part.

national logic, and one for any registers. Such a two-process behavioral description of the datapath is shown in Figure 5.11.

The first process in Figure 5.11 describes the datapath's combinational logic, whose inputs can be seen from Figure 5.10 to be *Cnt_s* and *Cnt*, which therefore appear in the process' sensitivity list. The body of the process consists of two IF statements. The first IF statement describes the behavior of the datapath output *CntNext*, including the behavior of the decrementer and the 2x1 mux. The second IF statement describes the behavior of the datapath output *Cnt_eq0*, essentially just describing a comparator with *0*. Notice that those two IF statements could have appeared in opposite order but would have still described the same behavior.

The second process in Figure 5.11 describes the datapath's register. When the clock is rising and the register load signal is asserted, the process updates the current signal value with the next value. Notice that reset behavior is included for the register, even though such behavior isn't strictly necessary for the correct operation of this particular datapath operation. The reset was included to follow good modeling practice, which involves always including reset behavior for every register. Also notice that only the *Clk* signal appears in the process sensitivity list, as the register is synchronous and thus is only updated on (rising) clock edges.

The controller's FSM would also be described using two processes, one for the combinational part, and one for the register, as was done in Chapter 3, and as shown in Figure 5.12.

Therefore, the controller and datapath description consists of four processes, two for the datapath (one for combinational logic, one for registers), and two for the controller (one for combinational logic, and one for registers), as shown in Figure 5.13. Those four processes appear in a single architecture. The datapath processes and controller processes communicate through the signals *Cnt_eq0*, *Cnt_s*, and *Cnt_ld*. The other signals are declared either for exclusive use of the datapath (*Cnt, CntNext*) or the controller (*Currstate, Nextstate*).

```
...
ARCHITECTURE CtrlDpBeh OF LaserTimer IS
   -- Shared signals
   SIGNAL Cnt_eq0, Cnt_s, Cnt_ld: std_logic;
   -- Datapath signals
   SIGNAL Cnt, CntNext: std_logic_vector(1 DOWNTO 0);
BEGIN
   ------ Datapath processes ------
   DPCombLogic: PROCESS (Cnt_s, Cnt)
   BEGIN
      IF (Cnt_s = '1') THEN
         CntNext <= "10";
      ELSE
         CntNext <= Cnt - "01";
      END IF;
      IF (Cnt = "00") THEN
         Cnt_eq0 <= '1';
      ELSE
         Cnt_eq0 <= '0';
      END IF;
   END PROCESS DPCombLogic;

   DpRegs: PROCESS (Clk)
   BEGIN
      IF (Clk = '1' AND Clk'EVENT) THEN
         IF (Rst = '1') THEN
            Cnt <= "00";
         ELSIF (Cnt_ld = '1') THEN
            Cnt <= CntNext;
         END IF;
      END IF;
   END PROCESS DpRegs;
...
```

Figure 5.11 Two-process description of a datapath.

```
ARCHITECTURE CtrlDpBeh OF LaserTimer IS
   ...
   -- Controller state signals
   TYPE Statetype IS (S_Off, S_On);
   SIGNAL Currstate, Nextstate: Statetype;
BEGIN   ...
   ------ Controller processes ------
   CtrlCombLogic: PROCESS (Currstate, Cnt_eq0, b)
   BEGIN
      CASE Currstate IS
         WHEN S_Off =>
            x <= '0'; Cnt_s <= '1'; Cnt_ld <= '1';
            IF (b = '0') THEN
               Nextstate <= S_Off;
            ELSE
               Nextstate <= S_On;
            END IF;
         WHEN S_On =>
            x <= '1'; Cnt_s <= '0'; Cnt_ld <= '1';
            IF (Cnt_eq0 = '1') THEN
               Nextstate <= S_Off;
            ELSE
               Nextstate <= S_On;
            END IF;
      END CASE;
   END PROCESS CtrlCombLogic;

   CtrlRegs: PROCESS (Clk)
   BEGIN
      IF (Clk = '1' AND Clk'EVENT) THEN
         IF (Rst = '1') THEN
            Currstate <= S_Off;
         ELSE
            Currstate <= Nextstate;
         END IF;
      END IF;
   END PROCESS CtrlRegs;
```

Figure 5.12 Two-process controller description.

```
LIBRARY ieee;
USE ieee.std_logic_1164.ALL;
USE ieee.std_logic_unsigned.ALL;

ENTITY LaserTimer IS
    PORT (b: IN std_logic;
          x: OUT std_logic;
          Clk, Rst: IN std_logic );
END LaserTimer;

ARCHITECTURE CtrlDpBeh OF LaserTimer IS
    -- Shared signals
    SIGNAL Cnt_eq0, Cnt_s, Cnt_ld: std_logic;
    -- Datapath signals
    SIGNAL Cnt, CntNext: std_logic_vector(1 DOWNTO 0);
    -- Controller state signals
    TYPE Statetype IS (S_Off, S_On);
    SIGNAL Currstate, Nextstate: Statetype;
BEGIN
    ------ Datapath processes ------
    DPCombLogic: PROCESS (Cnt_s, Cnt) ...
    END PROCESS DPCombLogic;

    DpRegs: PROCESS (Clk) ...
    END PROCESS DpRegs;

    ------ Controller processes ------
    CtrlCombLogic: PROCESS (Currstate, Cnt_eq0, b) ...
    END PROCESS CtrlCombLogic;

    CtrlRegs: PROCESS (Clk) ...
    END PROCESS CtrlRegs;

    END CtrlDpBeh;
```

Figure 5.13 Controller and datapath descriptions, consisting of two processes for the datapath, and two for the controller.

5.3 DESCRIBING A STATE MACHINE USING ONE PROCESS

Section 5.1 described how to describe a high-level state machine using two processes, using one process for combinational logic, and a second process for registers, as summarized in Figure 5.14(a). The two-process description required two signals for each register, a current signal, and a next signal.

A one-process description of a high-level state machine is also possible, and is quite commonly used. A one-process description is highlighted in Figure 5.14(b). In addition to using only one process, the description uses only one signal per register, rather than two signals per register. A one-process description thus has advantages of simplicity and improved readability.

Figure 5.15 provides a complete one-process description of the HLSM for the earlier laser-timer example. The process is sensitive only to the clock signal. If the clock is rising, the process checks whether the reset input is asserted, in which case the process resets all registers (the state register, and explicitly declared registers in the HLSM). If the reset is not asserted, then the process executes the HLSM's state actions based on the state signal's value, and sets the next state signal value according to the HLSM transitions.

```
ARCHITECTURE HLSM OF LaserTimer IS
   TYPE Statetype IS (S_Off, S_On);
   SIGNAL Currstate, Nextstate: Statetype;
   SIGNAL Cnt, CntNext: std_logic_vector(1 DOWNTO 0);
BEGIN
   CombLogic: PROCESS (Currstate, Cnt, b)...
   END PROCESS CombLogic;

   Regs: PROCESS (Clk) ...
   END PROCESS Regs;

END HLSM;
```

(a)

```
ARCHITECTURE HLSMOneProcess OF LaserTimer IS
   TYPE Statetype IS (S_Off, S_On);
   SIGNAL State: Statetype;
   SIGNAL Cnt: std_logic_vector(1 DOWNTO 0);
BEGIN
   PROCESS (Clk) ...
   END PROCESS;
END HLSMOneProcess;
```

(b)

Figure 5.14 Alternative approaches for describing a high-level state machine: (a) two-process description, (b) one-process description.

```
...
ARCHITECTURE HLSMOneProcess OF LaserTimer IS
   TYPE Statetype IS (S_Off, S_On);
   SIGNAL State: Statetype;
   SIGNAL Cnt: std_logic_vector(1 DOWNTO 0);
BEGIN
   PROCESS (Clk)
   BEGIN
      IF (Clk = '1' AND Clk'EVENT) THEN
         IF (Rst = '1') THEN
            State <= S_Off;
            Cnt <= "00";
         ELSE
            CASE State IS
               WHEN S_Off =>
                  x <= '0';
                  Cnt <= "10";
                  IF (b = '0') THEN
                     State <= S_Off;
                  ELSE
                     State <= S_On;
                  END IF;
               WHEN S_On =>
                  x <= '1';
                  Cnt <= Cnt - "01";
                  IF (Cnt = "00") THEN
                     State <= S_Off;
                  ELSE
                     State <= S_On;
                  END IF;
            END CASE;
         END IF;
      END IF;
   END PROCESS;
END HLSMOneProcess;
```

Figure 5.15 One-process description of a high-level state machine.

Compared to the two-process description shown in Figure 5.4 and Figure 5.5, the one-process description in Figure 5.15 is clearly simpler and easier to read. Why then was a two-process description introduced? The main reason relates to timing. The one-process description of Figure 5.15 does not exactly match the timing of the HLSM in Figure 5.1(b). In particular, the HLSM's behavior is such that changes to the HLSM inputs (i.e., to input b) would be seen by the HLSM immediately, and thus a change could influence the next state on the rising clock edge immediately following the change. Such behavior is accurately reflected by the two-process description, as shown in the waveforms of Figure 5.16(a), because the combinational logic process is independent of the clock signal. In contrast, the one-process description of Figure 5.15 is synchronous, meaning the process only checks the value of b on a rising clock edge, and thus a change cannot influence the next state until *two* rising clock edges after the change, as shown

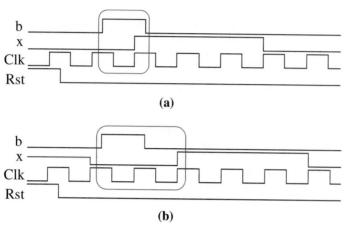

(a)

(b)

Figure 5.16 Timing differences between different descriptions: (a) In the two-process description, a change in *b* appearing sufficiently before a rising clock edge sets up the next state according to the new value of *b*, (b) In the one-process synchronous description, *b*'s value is only checked on rising clock edges, and thus a change in *b* is not noticed until the next rising edge, meaning the new value of *b* doesn't impact the next state until *two* rising clock edges after *b* changes.

in Figure 5.16(b). The one-process description thus introduces some delay into the system's behavior.

Introducing such delay is not necessarily a bad thing. In many systems, the extra cycle delay may represent an insignificant change. For example, in Figure 5.16, both waveforms ultimately represent acceptable behavior of the three-cycles-high laser timer system—the output stays high for exactly three clock cycles after a button press. For that system, it is not important if the three cycles are shifted in time by one cycle; what's important is that the output stays high for exactly three cycles. The insignificance of delays in detecting input changes is further illustrated by the fact that external inputs are typically fed through a series of flip-flops in order to isolate circuits from flip-flop metastability issues—that series of flip-flops introduces several cycles of delay itself.

Therefore, a one-process synchronous description is actually a reasonable and popular approach to describing a HLSM during RTL design. If the extra cycle for reading inputs does not pose a timing problem, the one-process description yields simpler and easier-to-read descriptions.

Actually, a one-process description need not differ in timing from a two-process description. The one-process description of Figure 5.15 was fully synchronous, being sensitive only to the clock signal, thus essentially representing a complex register. An alternative one-process description can maintain the asynchronous combinational functionality of the system, while also describing the synchronous register part. Such an alternative one-process description is shown in Figure 5.17. The description just merges the functionality of the two processes of

```
ARCHITECTURE HLSMOneProcess2 OF LaserTimer IS
    TYPE Statetype IS (S_Off, S_On);
    SIGNAL Currstate, Nextstate: Statetype;
    SIGNAL Cnt, Cnt_Next: std_logic_vector(1 DOWNTO 0);
BEGIN
    PROCESS (Clk, Currstate, b)
    BEGIN
        CASE Currstate IS
            WHEN S_Off =>
                x <= '0';
                Cnt_Next <= "10";
                IF (b = '0') THEN
                    Nextstate <= S_Off;
                ELSE
                    Nextstate <= S_On;
                END IF;
            WHEN S_On =>
                x <= '1';
                Cnt_Next <= Cnt - "01";
                IF (Cnt = "00") THEN
                    Nextstate <= S_Off;
                ELSE
                    Nextstate <= S_On;
                END IF;
        END CASE;

        IF (Clk = '1' AND Clk'EVENT) THEN
            IF (Rst = '1') THEN
                Currstate <= S_Off;
                Cnt <= "00";
            ELSE
                Currstate <= Nextstate;
                Cnt <= Cnt_Next;
            END IF;
        END IF;
    END PROCESS;
END HLSMOneProcess2;
```

Figure 5.17 Alternative, non-standard one-process description of a high-level state machine. The description merges the two-process description into a single process, maintaining separate combinational and register parts within that single process.

Figure 5.4 and Figure 5.5 into one process. The description uses two signals per register as in the two-process description, merges the sensitivity lists into one process, and contains a case statement for the combinational part and an IF statement for the register part. This description in Figure 5.17 has exactly the same behavior as the two processes in Figure 5.4 and Figure 5.5, reflecting the target architecture of Figure 5.2, and yielding the waveforms in Figure 5.16(a).

However, the merged one-process description is not a standard method for RTL description. While the authors verified that the description does synthesize correctly using two of the most commonly used commercial RTL synthesis tools, some tools may not handle that description properly. Thus, the authors do not presently recommend the one-process modeling approach for general use.

The same two-process versus one-process discussion applies as equally to FSMs as it does to HLSMs. Specifically, an FSM can be described using one process. The most common one-process FSM description approach uses the same structure as the process in Figure 5.15, having only the state register and no additional registers. The process uses a single signal for the state register, a process sensitive to the clock signal, and a single IF statement containing a reset part and an actions/transitions case statement part.

Furthermore, the same discussion regarding the alternative one-process description applies. An alternative one-process FSM description merely merges the two-processes into one processes, having two signals per register, merged sensitivity lists, and two distinct parts within the process, namely a combinational part, and a register part. However, this process, while resulting in correct circuits from popular synthesis tools, is non-standard and may not synthesize to correct circuits with some synthesis tools.

5.4 IMPROVING TIMING REALISM

[SIMUL] AFTER CLAUSES

Real components do not compute their outputs instantly after their inputs change. Instead, real components have delay—after inputs change, the correct outputs do not appear until some time later. For example, suppose the comparator in the datapath of Figure 5.9 has a delay of 7 ns. In order to obtain a more accurate RTL simulation of the controller and datapath in that figure, a description could be extended to include such delays. Figure 5.18 shows how the description of Figure 5.11 could be extended to include a 7 ns delay for the comparator component, by using AFTER clauses.

An *AFTER* clause is a clause that can be added to a signal assignment statement. The clause consists of the word "AFTER" followed by a time expression, which must evaluate to a time type. Including an AFTER clause indicates the amount of time in the future (relative to the present time) at which the signal update should occur. For this example, the two assignments to *Cnt_eq0*, which model the datapath's comparator, have been extended with AFTER clauses indicating a 7 ns delay. To more fully model the datapath component delays, AFTER clauses would also be added to the two *CntNext* assignments, modeling the delay of the mux and the decrementer.

Delays might be estimated from components existing in the component library that will be used in an implementation. Such delays are quite commonly included for low-level components like gates, muxes, registers, and so on.

```
...
DPCombLogic: PROCESS (Cnt_s, Cnt)
BEGIN
    IF (Cnt_s = '1') THEN
        CntNext <= "10";
    ELSE
        CntNext <= Cnt - "01";
    END IF;
    IF (Cnt = "00") THEN
        Cnt_eq0 <= '1' AFTER 7 NS;
    ELSE
        Cnt_eq0 <= '0' AFTER 7 NS;
    END IF;
END PROCESS DPCombLogic;
...
```

Figure 5.18 Including a component's delay in a description.

Including such delays in a description results in better timing accuracy during simulation, and can even detect timing problems. For example, if the clock period were shorter than the longest register-to-register delay in the datapath, the datapath with delays would compute incorrect results during simulation.

A tool synthesizing a circuit from a description having delays, like the description in Figure 5.18, would simply ignore the AFTER clauses. Those clauses serve to reflect the predicted timing behavior of the eventual implementation, and do *not* serve to guide the synthesis tool in creating that implementation.

Figure 5.19 illustrates the effect of including delays in a description. Figure 5.19(a) shows the simulation waveforms for the system when the comparator does not have any delay. That figure shows several internal signals, *Cnt*, *Cnt_eq0* (the comparator output), and *Currstate*. Figure 5.19(b) shows the simulation waveforms for the description having the 7 ns comparator delay. Notice that the comparator's output, *Cnt_eq0*, is slightly shifted to the right, due to the delay.

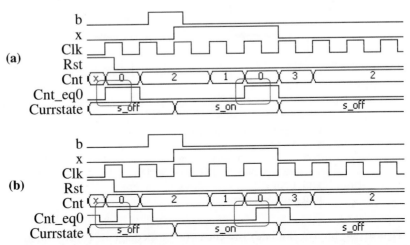

Figure 5.19 Simulation results: (a) without comparator delay, (b) with 7 ns delay.

5.5 ALGORITHMIC-LEVEL BEHAVIOR

In the early stages of design, a designer may want to describe a system's behavior at an even higher level of abstraction than the register-transfer level. Sometimes, the behavior is naturally described first as an algorithm. For example, consider a system that computes the sum of absolute differences (SAD) of the corresponding elements of two 256-element arrays. Such a computation is useful in video compression to determine the difference between two video frames, for example. A SAD system block diagram appears in Figure 5.20(a). The system's algorithmic-level behavior is shown in Figure 5.20(b). The algorithm, which is written in pseudo-code and not in any particular language, indicates that the system is activated when the input *Go* becomes '*1*'. The algorithm then generates array indices from 0 to 255, one at a time. For each index, the algorithm computes the absolute value of the difference of the two array elements for that index, and adds that value to a running sum variable. The algorithm then writes the final sum to the system's output. Notice how simple and clear an algorithm-level description can be. A designer may wish to verify the correctness of the algorithm, before proceeding to design the system at the RT level.

Figure 5.21 shows an algorithmic-level description of the SAD system's behavior. Although the two 256-element arrays A and B are external to the SAD system itself as shown in Figure 5.20(a), the algorithmic-level description initially declares those two arrays as part of the SAD architecture. Although not necessary, such declaration makes the initial description easier to create. Details of those array declarations will be described shortly.

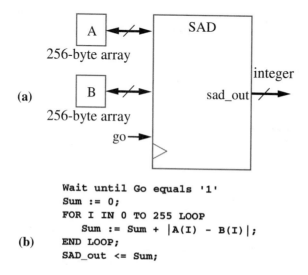

Figure 5.20 Sum of absolute differences: (a) block diagram, (b) algorithm.

```
LIBRARY ieee;
USE ieee.std_logic_1164.ALL;
USE ieee.std_logic_signed.ALL;

ENTITY SAD IS
   PORT (Go: IN std_logic;
           SAD_out: OUT integer;
           Clk, Rst: IN std_logic );
END SAD;

ARCHITECTURE SAD_Alg OF SAD IS
   TYPE SADArrayType IS ARRAY(0 TO 255)
                          OF std_logic_vector(7 DOWNTO 0);
     -- somehow declare A and B here
BEGIN
   PROCESS
      VARIABLE Sum: integer;
   BEGIN
      IF (NOT(Go='1')) THEN
         WAIT UNTIL Go='1';
      END IF;
      Sum := 0;
      FOR I IN 0 TO 255 LOOP
         Sum := Sum + Conv_Integer(ABS(A(I) - B(I)));
      END LOOP;
      WAIT FOR 50 ns;
      SAD_out <= Sum;
   END PROCESS;

END SAD_Alg;
```

Figure 5.21 Sum of absolute differences algorithmic-level description.

The description consists of one process. The process contents look very similar to the algorithm in Figure 5.20(b). A variable *Sum*, declared as an integer, is used to keep the sum of absolute differences. **Integer** is a pre-defined data type in VHDL that can be used when declaring variables or signals. A FOR loop generates indices 0 to 255. The function *ABS*, defined in the package *ieee.std_logic_signed.ALL* for *std_logic_vector*, is used to compute the absolute value. The *Conv_Integer* function, also defined in that package, is used to convert the *std_logic_vector* representation of the absolute value of the difference into an integer, which can then be added to the *Sum* variable.

The description's use of the two WAIT statements require some discussion. The statement "*WAIT FOR 50 ns;*" appears to create some delay (albeit a rather short one) between the time that *Go* becomes '1' and the time that the computed SAD value appears at the output. Including a WAIT statement at the end of the process also prevents an infinite simulation loop in which the process repeatedly executes without ever suspending.

The first WAIT statement, "*WAIT UNTIL Go='1';*", suspends the process, and resumes when *Go* changes to '*1*'. The word "changes" is critical in the previous sentence. If *Go* is '*1*' when that WAIT statement is reached during execution, the process still suspends at that WAIT statement. The process stays suspended at that statement until *Go* changes to '*0*' and then changes back to '*1*'. This behavior of a WAIT UNTIL statement is somewhat counterintuitive, as many designers make the mistake of believing that if *Go* was '*1*' when reaching the statement, execution will simply proceed to the next statement without the process suspending.

The description therefore uses an IF statement to achieve the desired behavior of the process proceeding to compute the SAD if *Go* is already '*1*'. The IF statement proceeds to execute the WAIT statement only if *Go* is not already '*1*'; otherwise, execution proceeds on to the SAD calculation.

The last aspect of the description is the declaration of the arrays *A* and *B*. The type declaration of Figure 5.21 defines an array type of 256 8-bit elements. The arrays can be declared as signals of that type, e.g., "*signal A, B: SADArrayType;*". However, because this algorithmic-level description initially includes the arrays internal to the SAD so that the SAD can be easily created and tested, the arrays should be initialized with some values. One initialization method would use a second process to write values into the arrays.

However, for initial quick testing purposes of just one set of array values, the description could instead initialize the signal values in the signal declaration itself, as shown in Figure 5.22. The initialization syntax is the same as for a constant declaration, using the "*:=*" symbol followed by the initial value (or values). The initialization syntax is the same for a signal declaration, variable declaration, or constant declaration. A constant declaration obviously must be initialized, while initialization is optional for signal and variable declarations.

The initial values used in Figure 5.22 are arbitrary. For the shown values, however, the computed SAD should equal four, because elements 0, 4, 248, and 252 are the only differing elements, and they each differ by just 1 ("*00000000*" versus "*00000001*").

Figure 5.23 provides a simple test vector process for the algorithm-level SAD description. The process resets the SAD component (even though the SAD component's description does nothing in response to that reset), pulses *Go_s*, waits for some time, and then checks that the computed SAD equals four. Simulation waveforms are shown in Figure 5.24. Note that the SAD output is initially a large negative number, due to the output not having been explicitly set to some value when the SAD process first executed. A better description would set the output to some value, likely during reset.

```
...
ARCHITECTURE SAD_Alg OF SAD IS
   TYPE SADArrayType IS ARRAY(0 TO 255)
                       OF std_logic_vector(7 DOWNTO 0);
   SIGNAL A: SADArrayType := (
      "00000000", "00000001", "00000010", "00000011",
      "00000000", "00000001", "00000010", "00000011",
      ...
      "00000000", "00000001", "00000010", "00000011",
      "00000000", "00000001", "00000010", "00000011" );
   SIGNAL B: SADArrayType := (
      "00000001", "00000001", "00000010", "00000011",
      "00000001", "00000001", "00000010", "00000011",
      "00000000", "00000001", "00000010", "00000011",
      ...
      "00000000", "00000001", "00000010", "00000011",
      "00000001", "00000001", "00000010", "00000011",
      "00000001", "00000001", "00000010", "00000011" );
BEGIN
   PROCESS
      VARIABLE Sum: integer;
   BEGIN
      IF (NOT(Go='1')) THEN
         WAIT UNTIL Go='1';
      END IF;
      Sum := 0;
      FOR I IN 0 TO 255 LOOP
         Sum := Sum + Conv_Integer(ABS(A(I) - B(I)));
      END LOOP;
      WAIT FOR 50 ns;
      SAD_out <= Sum;
   END PROCESS;

END SAD_Alg;
```

Figure 5.22 Declaring the SAD arrays as initialized signals.

```
...
    VectorProcess: PROCESS
    BEGIN
       Rst_s <= '1';
       Go_s <= '0';
       WAIT UNTIL Clk_s='1' and Clk_s'EVENT;

       Rst_s <= '0';
       Go_s <= '1';
       WAIT UNTIL Clk_s='1' and Clk_s'EVENT;

       Go_s <= '0';
       WAIT UNTIL Clk_s='1' and Clk_s'EVENT;

       WAIT FOR 60 ns;
       ASSERT (SAD_out_s = 4) REPORT "SAD incorrect";

       WAIT;
    END PROCESS VectorProcess;
...
```

Figure 5.23 Simple testbench vector process for the SAD algorithmic-level description.

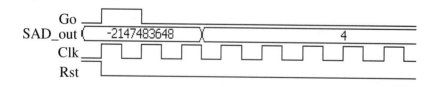

Figure 5.24 Waveforms for the SAD algorithmic-level description.

5.6 TOP-DOWN DESIGN—CONVERTING ALGORITHMIC-LEVEL BEHAVIOR TO RTL

Once satisfied that an algorithm is correct, a designer may wish to proceed to convert the algorithm-level behavior to an RTL description, as a means of moving towards an implementation of the system. The algorithm of Figure 5.21 can be recaptured as the HLSM shown in Figure 5.25. The HLSM can then be described as shown in Figure 5.26. The HLSM can be tested using the same testbench as in Figure 5.23, except that the testbench should wait longer than just 60 ns for the SAD output to appear. By counting the number of HLSM states that must be visited to compute the SAD, one can determine a waiting time of (256*2+3) * (20 ns), where 20 ns is the clock period. Figure 5.27 provides the resulting waveforms, showing several internal signals to better demonstrate the HLSM's behavior during simulation.

Local registers: sum, sad_reg (32 bits); i (9 bits)

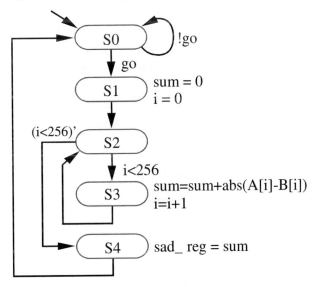

Figure 5.25 HLSM for the SAD system.

```
...
    TYPE Statetype IS (S0,S1,S2,S3,S4);
    SIGNAL State_reg: Statetype;
    SIGNAL Sum_reg, SAD_reg: integer;
    SIGNAL I_reg: integer;
BEGIN
    PROCESS(Clk)
    BEGIN
        IF (Clk='1' AND Clk'EVENT) THEN
            IF (Rst='1') THEN
                State_reg <= S0;
                Sum_reg   <= 0;
                SAD_reg   <= 0;
                I_reg     <= 0;
            ELSE
                CASE (State_reg) IS
                    WHEN S0 =>
                        IF (Go='1') THEN
                            State_reg <= S1;
                        ELSE
                            State_reg <= S0;
                        END IF;
                    WHEN S1 =>
                        Sum_reg <= 0;
                        I_reg   <= 0;
                        State_reg <= S2;

                    WHEN S2 =>
                        IF (NOT(I_reg = 255)) THEN
                            State_reg <= S3;
                        ELSE
                            State_reg <= S4;
                        END IF;
                    WHEN S3 =>
                        Sum_reg <= Sum_reg +
                            Conv_Integer(ABS(A(I_reg)-B(I_reg)));
                        I_reg <= I_reg + 1;
                        State_reg <= S2;
                    WHEN S4 =>
                        SAD_reg <= Sum_reg;
                        State_reg <= S0;
                    WHEN OTHERS =>
                        State_reg <= S0;
                END CASE;
            END IF;
        END IF;
    END PROCESS;
    SAD_out <= SAD_reg;
...
```

Figure 5.26 Description of the HLSM for the SAD system.

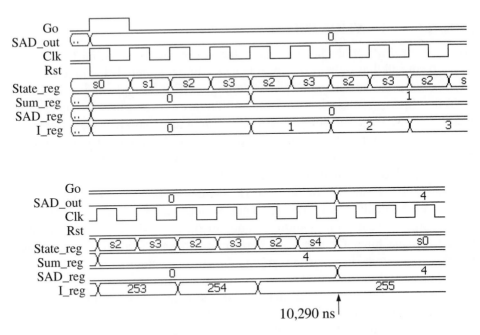

Figure 5.27 Waveforms for HLSM of the SAD system.

[SYNTH] AUTOMATED SYNTHESIS FROM THE ALGORITHMIC-LEVEL

Several commercial tools, known as *behavioral synthesis* or *high-level synthesis* tools, have been introduced in the 1990s and 2000s intending to automatically synthesize algorithmic-code to RTL code or even directly to circuits. Such tools have not yet been adopted as widely as RTL synthesis tools. Each tool imposes strong requirements and restrictions on the algorithmic-level code that may be synthesized, and those requirements and restrictions vary tremendously across tools. The quality of RTL code or circuits created from such tools also varies tremendously. Nevertheless, behavioral synthesis tools represent an interesting direction and may prove increasingly useful in coming years.

[SIMUL] SIMULATION SPEED

Higher-level descriptions not only have the advantage of requiring less time to create them and thus of being more suitable for initial system behavior definition, but also have the advantage of faster simulation. For example, the algorithmic-level description of the sum-of-absolute-differences system may simulate faster than an HLSM description of that system, which in turn may simulate faster than a lower-level description like a gate-level description. When the system's *Go* input becomes *'1'*, the algorithmic-level description resumes a process that then executes a FOR loop that involves only a few thousand calculations in total to compute the output result. In contrast, the HLSM description would require tens of thousands of calculations by the simulator, which must suspend and resume the HLSM process nearly one thousand times in order to simulate the clock-controlled state machine of that process, performing dozens of calculations each time the process resumes in order to compute the current output values and the next state. For a small testbench, the simulation speed difference may not be noticeable. However, for a large testbench, or for a system comprised of hundreds or thousands of sub-systems, the simulation speed difference may become quite significant. It is not unusual for system simulations to run for hours. Thus, a 10 times difference in simulation speed may mean the difference between a 10-20 minute simulation versus a 2-3 hour simulation; a 100 times slower simulation could take days. Thus, high-level descriptions are favored early in the design process, when system behavior is being defined and refined. Low-level descriptions are necessary to achieve an implementation. High-level descriptions are also useful when integrating components in a large system, to see if those components interact properly from a behavioral perspective—the fast simulation speed allows for testing of a large variety of component interaction scenarios. Lower-level descriptions would be more suitable to verify detailed timing correctness of such large systems, as their slower simulation speed allows for only relatively few scenarios to be examined. For example, a system consisting of several microprocessor components described at a high level might be able to simulate minutes of microprocessor execution in a few hours, but might only be able to simulate a few seconds of microprocessor execution if described at a low level.

We previously showed how state machines could be modeled using two processes where one process was combinational, or using one process where that process was sensitive only to a clock signal. The latter will simulate much faster than the former, due to fewer process resumes and suspends. The difference may not be noticeable for small systems, but if a system contains hundreds or thousands of state machines, the difference can become quite significant.

5.7 MEMORY

Desired storage may initially be described merely using signals declared within a system's architecture, as was done in the SAD example of the previous section and as illustrated in Figure 5.28(a). However, refining the description towards an implementation may mean creating a description with that storage described as a separate memory component, as in Figure 5.28(b).

Describing memory separately begins by creating a new entity representing a memory. A description for a simple read-only memory (ROM) appears in Figure 5.29. The memory description has an input port for the address, and an output port for the data. In this case, the bitwidth of those ports are the same, but they obviously can be different depending on the memory size and width. The memory contains a constant representing the ROM contents. In the figure, the ROM represented is for memory A of the SAD example; a similar description would be created for memory B, with different ROM contents. The description contains a process that is sensitive to the address input, and that simply outputs the appropriate data for the given address.

Figure 5.30 shows the HLSM for the SAD example, modified to access the external memory components. Rather than simply access A and B values, the HLSM must now set its address outputs *A_addr* and *B_addr*, and then use the returned data inputs *A_data* and *B_data*. Furthermore, because the HLSM is fully synchronous due to modeling it using a single process sensitive only to the clock signal, the HLSM requires an extra state, *S3a*. Although the A and B memories will be combinational components, the extra state is necessary because the *A_data* and *B_data* inputs will only be sampled on clock edges due to the fully synchronous HLSM model being used.

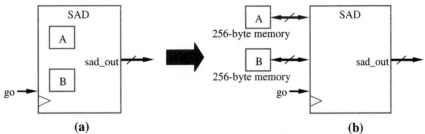

(a)   (b)

Figure 5.28   A more accurate system description may create memory as a separate component.

```
...
LIBRARY ieee;
USE ieee.std_logic_1164.ALL;
USE ieee.std_logic_unsigned.ALL;
USE ieee.std_logic_arith.ALL;

ENTITY SAD_MemA IS
    PORT (addr: IN std_logic_vector(7 DOWNTO 0);
          data: OUT std_logic_vector(7 DOWNTO 0) );
END SAD_MemA;

ARCHITECTURE SAD_MemA_Beh OF SAD_MemA IS
    TYPE SADArrayType IS ARRAY(0 TO 255)
                        OF std_logic_vector(7 DOWNTO 0);
    CONSTANT MemA: SADArrayType := (
        "00000000", "00000001", "00000010", "00000011",
        "00000000", "00000001", "00000010", "00000011",
        ...
        "00000000", "00000001", "00000010", "00000011",
        "00000000", "00000001", "00000010", "00000011" );

BEGIN
    PROCESS(addr)
    BEGIN
        data <= MemA(Conv_Integer(addr));
    END PROCESS;

END SAD_MemA_Beh;
...
```

Figure 5.29 Description of a simple read-only memory.

Local registers: sum, sad_reg (32 bits); i (9 bits)

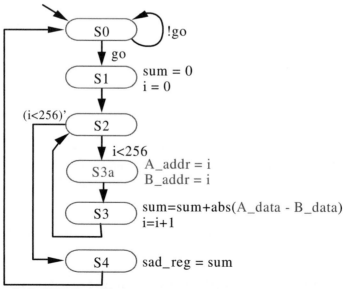

Figure 5.30 SAD HLSM modified to access the external memory components.

Figure 5.31 shows the first part of a description of the new SAD HLSM that uses memory components. The entity declaration now includes the ports for interfacing with the external memory components. Furthermore, the description now defines a function *AbsDiff* that computes the absolute value of the difference of two logic vectors. The previous description uses the *ABS* function defined in the *std_logic_signed* package. However, the new description uses *std_logic_unsigned*, as the address and data lines interfacing with the memory components use unsigned vectors. Because both packages cannot be used in the same entity, *ABS* cannot be used, and thus the new description defines the AbsDiff function in a way that does not result in an intermediate negative value.

Figure 5.32 shows the second part of the new HLSM description. The part shown illustrates the new state *S3a*, corresponding to the HLSM of Figure 5.30. Notice how the access to items *A* and *B* is now completely through address and data ports. Also notice that state *S3* now calls function *AbsDiff* rather than *ABS*. A synthesis tool would replace that function call by the contents of the function itself. In other words, the description could have included *AbsDiff*'s IF-THEN-ELSE statement directly in state *S3*. However, using the function leads to improved readability of the HLSM.

```
...
USE ieee.std_logic_unsigned.ALL;
USE ieee.std_logic_arith.ALL;
...
ENTITY SAD IS
   PORT (Go: IN std_logic;
         A_addr: OUT std_logic_vector(7 DOWNTO 0);
         A_data: IN std_logic_vector(7 DOWNTO 0);
         B_addr: OUT std_logic_vector(7 DOWNTO 0);
         B_data: IN std_logic_vector(7 DOWNTO 0);
         SAD_out: OUT integer;
         Clk, Rst: IN std_logic );
END SAD;

ARCHITECTURE SAD_HLSM OF SAD IS
   TYPE Statetype IS (S0,S1,S2,S3a,S3,S4);
   ...


   FUNCTION AbsDiff(A, B: std_logic_vector(7 DOWNTO 0))
      RETURN integer IS
   BEGIN
      IF (A > B) THEN
         RETURN(Conv_Integer(A-B));
      ELSE
         RETURN(Conv_Integer(B-A));
      END IF;
   END FUNCTION;
```

Figure 5.31 SAD HLSM description with separate memory (part 1).

```
...
BEGIN
    PROCESS(Clk)
    BEGIN
        IF (Clk='1' AND Clk'EVENT) THEN
            IF (Rst='1') THEN
                ...
            ELSE
                CASE (State_reg) IS
                    ...
                    WHEN S2 =>
                        IF (NOT(I_reg = 255)) THEN
                            State_reg <= S3a;
                        ELSE
                            State_reg <= S4;
                        END IF;
                    WHEN S3a =>
                        A_addr <=
                            Conv_Std_Logic_Vector(I_reg,8);
                        B_addr <=
                            Conv_Std_Logic_Vector(I_reg,8);
                        State_reg <= S3;
                    WHEN S3 =>
                        Sum_reg <= Sum_reg +
                            AbsDiff(A_data, B_data);
                        I_reg <= I_reg + 1;
                        State_reg <= S2;
                    ...;
                END CASE;
            END IF;
        END IF;
    END PROCESS;
    SAD_out <= SAD_reg;

END SAD_HLSM;
...
```

Figure 5.32 SAD HLSM description with separate memory (part 2).

Figure 5.33 shows the first part of a testbench for the SAD system with separate memory components. The testbench declares three components: the SAD component, the memory *A* component, and the memory *B* component. The testbench also declares the signals needed for connecting those components together, and then connects them using port maps. Note that a testbench can instantiate multiple components for testing, rather than instantiating just one component. To the extent possible, designers should always test components separately, before testing them together in a single testbench.

Figure 5.34 shows the second part of the testbench, having the clock and vector processes. The vector process is similar to the process of the previous SAD HLSM without external memory components, except that the process must wait longer for the SAD output to appear, due to the extra state in the HLSM. Thus, rather than waiting (256*2+3) * (20 ns), the process waits (256*3+3) * (20 ns).

```
...
ARCHITECTURE TBarch OF Testbench IS
    COMPONENT SAD IS
        PORT (Go: IN std_logic;
              A_addr: OUT std_logic_vector(7 DOWNTO 0);
              A_data: IN std_logic_vector(7 DOWNTO 0);
              B_addr: OUT std_logic_vector(7 DOWNTO 0);
              B_data: IN std_logic_vector(7 DOWNTO 0);
              SAD_out: OUT integer;
              Clk, Rst: IN std_logic );
    END COMPONENT;

    COMPONENT SAD_MemA IS
        PORT (addr: IN std_logic_vector(7 DOWNTO 0);
              data: OUT std_logic_vector(7 DOWNTO 0) );
    END COMPONENT SAD_MemA;

    COMPONENT SAD_MemB IS
        PORT (addr: IN std_logic_vector(7 DOWNTO 0);
              data: OUT std_logic_vector(7 DOWNTO 0) );
    END COMPONENT SAD_MemB;

    SIGNAL Go_s: std_logic;
    SIGNAL A_addr_s, B_addr_s: std_logic_vector(7 DOWNTO 0);
    SIGNAL A_data_s, B_data_s: std_logic_vector(7 DOWNTO 0);
    SIGNAL SAD_out_s: integer;
    SIGNAL Clk_s, Rst_s: std_logic;

    SIGNAL ClkPeriod : TIME := 20 ns;

BEGIN
    CompToTest: SAD PORT MAP
        (Go_s, A_addr_s, A_data_s, B_addr_s, B_data_s,
         SAD_out_s, Clk_s, Rst_s);
    A_Mem: SAD_MemA PORT MAP (A_addr_s, A_data_s);
    B_Mem: SAD_MemB PORT MAP (B_addr_s, B_data_s);
```

Figure 5.33 SAD HLSM testbench with memory components (part 1).

...

```
ClkProcess: PROCESS
BEGIN
    Clk_s <= '0';
    WAIT FOR ClkPeriod/2;
    Clk_s <= '1';
    WAIT FOR ClkPeriod/2;
END PROCESS ClkProcess;

VectorProcess: PROCESS
BEGIN
    Rst_s <= '1';
    Go_s <= '0';
    WAIT UNTIL Clk_s='1' AND Clk_s'EVENT;

    Rst_s <= '0';
    Go_s <= '1';
    WAIT FOR (256*3 + 3)*ClkPeriod;
    ASSERT (SAD_out_s = 4) REPORT "SAD failed -- should equal 4";

    WAIT;
END PROCESS VectorProcess;
```

Figure 5.34 SAD HLSM testbench with memory components (part 2).

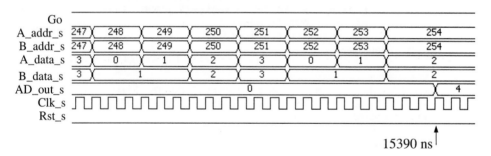

Figure 5.35 Waveforms for SAD HLSM with memory components.

The testbench in Figure 5.33 and Figure 5.34 has also been improved by declaring (in Figure 5.33) a constant named *ClkPeriod* to represent the clock's period of 20 ns, and using that constant (in Figure 5.34) in the clock and vector processes, rather than hardcoding the 20 ns value throughout. Declaring such a constant enables a designer to easily change the clock period just by changing one number, rather than having to change multiple numbers scattered throughout the code (and possibly forgetting to change the number in one place or changing a number when it should not have been changed). The constant declaration uses the type *TIME*, which consists of a number and a timescale like *ns* (nanoseconds).

Finally, Figure 5.35 shows waveforms generated from the testbench. Waveforms for the address and data signals now appear. The final SAD output also appears, although it appears later than in Figure 5.27, due to the extra state in the HLSM. Generally, converting a design from higher-levels to levels closer to an implementation yield increasing timing accuracy.

CHAPTER 6

VHDL Mini-Reference

6.1 BASIC SYNTAX

COMMENTS

VHDL *comments* begin with two hyphens, *"--"*, and continue until the end of the line. Comments can be used to provide annotations about VHDL code to provide designers with additional information regarding the code. All VHDL comments are single line comments, but may start on the same line following VHDL statements. Comments too long to fit on a single line can be split into multiple comments, one per line, beginning with *"--"* at the start of each line of the comment. VHDL comments do not affect the simulation or synthesis of a VHDL description, but are very useful to human readers.

Examples:

```
-- Example of a single line comment
A <= '0'; -- Reset condition

-- Comments that are long may be separated
-- into multiple lines. Each line of the
-- comment must begin with "--"
```

IDENTIFIERS

Identifiers are user-defined names within a VHDL description and are used to identify any user-defined object within a VHDL description. User-defined names, or identifiers, must start with a letter, optionally followed by any sequence of letters, numbers, and underscore characters, with the restrictions that two underscores cannot appear in a row and an underscore cannot be the last character of an identifier.

Examples:

```
A
B14
Wire_23
test_entity
```

Invalid Examples:

```
IN         -- reserved word
4x1Mux     -- does not begin with letter
_in4       -- does not begin with letter
Wire_      -- ends with underscore
Wire__23 -- includes two underscores in a row
```

LITERALS

A literal is the representation of a value of a specific type. Literals are used to assign specific values to signals, variables, constants, generics, etc. and within expressions that include a specific value.

Integers

An integer literal is a literal that defines a decimal integer number, consisting of one or more decimal digits. An integer literal can also include underscores to separate digits within the literal, with the restrictions that two underscores cannot appear in a row and an underscore cannot end the literal. Underscores have no effect on the value of the literal.

Examples:

```
123
45
1_450_891
```

Characters

A character literal is a literal that defines a single character, consisting of a single graphical character enclosed between two apostrophes. Character literals are used to represent the logic values '0' and '1', among others.

Examples:

```
'0'
'1'
'Z'
'A'
'_'
```

Strings

A string literal is a sequence of characters enclosed between two quotation marks. If a quotation mark needs to be part of the string literal itself, two quotation marks within the string literal can be used to represent the quotation mark within the literal. A string literal must fit on a single line. If longer string literals are needed, the concatenation operation can be used to concatenate multiple string literals on separate lines together.

Examples:

```
"Error: File not found."

"This string is very long and looks better" &
"when split into two strings on separate lines"

"""" -- A string containing a single quotation
```

Bit Strings

A bit string literal is used to specify a literal consisting of a sequence of bits. Bit string literals are important for assigning values to *bit_vector*, *std_logic_vector*, *signed*, and *unsigned* types, among others. A bit string literal is a sequence of digits enclosed between two quotation marks. A bit string literal can include underscores to separate digits within the literal, with the restrictions that two underscores cannot appear in a row and an underscore cannot end the literal. Underscores have no effect on the value of the literal.

A bit string literal can be specified in one of three bases, binary, octal, or hexadecimal, denoted by including the character '*B*', '*O*', or '*X*', respectively, immediately before the quotation beginning the literal value. When specifying a binary literal, the literal's digits are restricted to the 0 or 1. When specifying an octal literal, the literal's digits are limited to 0 through 7, and the value of the literal is the bit string equivalent obtained by replacing each octal digit with the corresponding three binary digits. When specifying an hexadecimal literal, the literal's digits are limited to 0 through 9 and A through F, and the value of the literal is the bit string equivalent obtained by replacing each hexadecimal digit with the corresponding four binary digits. Note that a bit string literal specified with an octal or hexadecimal base can only represent bit string literals with lengths that are multiples of three and four, respectively.

Examples:

```
-- The following examples all represent the
-- the same bit string literal
B"111111111111"
B"1111_1111_1111"
O"7777"
X"FFF"
```

RESERVED WORDS

A *reserved word*, also referred to as a *keyword*, is an identifier that has special significance in the language and may not be used as a user defined name within a VHDL description. The full list of VHDL reserved words is presented here in all uppercase letters. Note that VHDL is case insensitive, and thus lowercase or mixed case versions of the reserved words are still considered reserved words.

ABS	ACCESS	AFTER
ALIAS	ALL	AND
ARCHITECTURE	ARRAY	ASSERT
ATTRIBUTE	BEGIN	BLOCK
BODY	BUFFER	BUS
CASE	COMPONENT	CONFIGURATION
CONSTANT	DISCONNECT	DOWNTO
ELSE	ELSIF	END
ENTITY	EXIT	FILE
FOR	FUNCTION	GENERATE
GENERIC	GROUP	GUARDED
IF	IMPURE	IN
INERTIAL	INOUT	IS
LABEL	LIBRARY	LINKAGE
LITERAL	LOOP	MAP
MOD	NAND	NEW
NEXT	NOR	NOT
NULL	OF	ON
OPEN	OR	OTHERS
OUT	PACKAGE	PORT
POSTPONED	PROCEDURAL	PROCEDURE
PROCESS	PROTECTED	PURE
RANGE	RECORD	REFERENCE
REGISTER	REJECT	REM

REPORT	RETURN	ROL
ROR	SELECT	SEVERITY
SIGNAL	SHARED	SLA
SLL	SRA	SRL
SUBTYPE	THEN	TO
TRANSPORT	TYPE	UNAFFECTED
UNITS	UNTIL	USE
VARIABLE	WAIT	WHEN
WHILE	WITH	XNOR
XOR		

6.2 DECLARATIONS

ENTITY

```
ENTITY name IS
    ports
    generics
END name;
```

An ***entity declaration*** defines an entity's *interface* to the outside world, including the entity's name, inputs, and outputs. An entity declaration may also include the declaration of the entity's ports and generics, but are not required.

Ports

```
PORT (name: direction type;
      name: direction type);
```

The entity's inputs and outputs, known as ***ports*** appear in a list contained between the parentheses of the statement "*PORT ( );*". Semicolons separate each port in the list — note that the last port is not followed by a semicolon, since there is no following port from which to separate. Each port consists of a name, a direction (e.g., *IN*, *OUT*, or *INOUT*), and a type. Multiple ports of the same type and direction can be grouped together, where each port name is separated by a comma.

Example:

```
ENTITY And2 IS
    PORT (x: IN std_logic;
          y: IN std_logic;
```

```
            F: OUT std_logic);
    END And2;

    ENTITY And2 IS
        PORT (x,y: IN std_logic;
                F: OUT std_logic);
    END And2;
```

Generics

```
    GENERIC (name: type := default_value;
             name: type := default_value);
```

A *generic* is a constant value defined within an entity declaration that declares a generic constant. Unlike other constants, the value for a generic can be specified within a component instantiation and can vary across multiple instances of the component. The entity's generics appear in a list contained between the parentheses of the statement "*GENERIC ( );*". Semicolons separate each generic in the list — note that the last generic is not followed by a semicolon, since there is no following generics from which to separate. Each generic consists of a name, a type, and a default value for the generic.

Example:

```
    ENTITY Mux2 IS
        GENERIC (Width: integer := 4);
        -- Rest of entity declaration
    END Mux2;
```

Architecture Body

```
    ARCHITECTURE name OF entity_name IS
        declarative_part
    BEGIN
        statements_part
    END name;
```

An *architecture body* defines what is *inside* an entity. In other words, the architecture body describes the function of the entity, namely, how the entity's outputs are related to the entity's inputs. The architecture body declaration defines the architecture name and the entity name of the entity declaration of the design. Multiple architectures may exist for a single entity.

The architecture body includes two parts, the architecture declarative part and the architecture statements part. The architecture's declarative part incudes declarations of items that are available within the architecture and may include component, signal, constant, and type declarations, among others. The architecture's statement part includes the statements that define the internal operation of the design.

Example:

```
ARCHITECTURE And2_beh OF And2 IS
BEGIN

    PROCESS(x, y)
    BEGIN
        F <= x AND y;
    END PROCESS;

END And2_beh;
```

COMPONENT

```
COMPONENT name IS
    ports
    generics
END COMPONENT;
```

A *component* is an entity used within a circuit. A *component declaration* defines the component's name and the component's input and output ports, which all should be the same as they were in the component's original entity declaration.

Example:

```
COMPONENT And2 IS
    PORT (x: IN std_logic;
          y: IN std_logic;
          F: OUT std_logic);
END COMPONENT;
```

CONFIGURATION

```
CONFIGURATION name OF entity_name IS
    FOR architecture_name
```

```
        FOR instance_name: component_type
            USE ENTITY
                library.entity_name(architecture_name);
        END FOR;
    END FOR;
END name;
```

A *configuration declaration* defines the bindings between component instances and design entities. Configurations are most often used to select which architecture of an entity should be used during simulation. A single entity may have multiple architectures describing the entity's internal design. For example, Figure 2.23 shows a *BeltWarn* entity with two architectures, one behavioral, the other structural. However, during simulation, only one architecture can be used. While many simulators provide simple mechanisms for selecting which architecture to use, a configuration declaration can also be used to specify which architecture to use.

The configuration declaration begins by defining the configuration name and the entity that is being configured using the syntax, "*CONFIGURATION name OF entity_name IS*". As several architectures may exist for the entity being configured, the configuration must first specify which architecture of the entity is being configured using a block configuration. A *block configuration* defines the configuration for an architecture with the keyword *FOR* followed by the name of the architecture being configured. For example, the statement "*FOR TBarch*" defines the block configuration for the architecture *TBarch*. The block configuration may include zero or more component configurations between the block configuration's declaration and the "*END FOR;*" statement at the end of the block configuration.

A *component configuration* defines the bindings between the component instances within the specified architecture of the entity being configured and design entities that should be used for each of those components. In other words, a component configuration indicates which design entities should be used for a specific component instance. A component declaration begins with the keyword *FOR* followed by the component instance being configured and the type of component separate by a colon. For example, the component configuration "*FOR Comp-ToTest: BeltWarn*" declares a configuration for the component instance named *CompToTest* that is a *BeltWarn* component. A basic component configuration will include a single *USE* statement that indicates which design entity should be used for this component instance. The *USE* statement begins with "*USE ENTITY*" followed by the name of the library containing the design entity and the entity name separated by a period with the entity's architecture specified within parentheses after the entity name. For example, the statement "*USE ENTITY work.Belt-Warn(Behav);*" indicates that the *Behav* architecture of the entity *BeltWarn* within the *work* library should be used for the specified component instance. The library for the design entity is typically the working library, named *work*, that is used by a simulator for all user defined entities. The component configuration ends with the "*END FOR;*" statement.

The following configuration examples include two configuration declarations, named *CfgTestBeh* and *CfgTestStruct,* that demonstrate how to configure the test-bench of Figure 2.15 to simulate the *BeltWarn* design of Figure 2.23 using the *Behav* and *Circuit* architectures, respectively.

Examples:
```
-- Configuration specifying that the Behav
-- architecture of the BeltWarn entity
-- should be selected for CompToTest
CONFIGURATION CfgTestBeh OF Testbench IS
    FOR TBarch
        FOR CompToTest: BeltWarn
            USE ENTITY work.BeltWarn(Behav);
        END FOR;
    END FOR;
END CfgTestBeh;

-- Configuration specifying that the Circuit
-- architecture of the BeltWarn entity
-- should be selected for CompToTest
CONFIGURATION CfgTestStruct OF Testbench IS
    FOR TBarch
        FOR CompToTest: BeltWarn
            USE ENTITY work.BeltWarn(Circuit);
        END FOR;
    END FOR;
END CfgTestStruct;
```

CONSTANT

```
CONSTANT name: type := constant_value;
```

A *constant* is an object that represents a fixed value that cannot be changed after the constant declaration. A *constant declaration* statement must specify the constant name, constant type, and define the fixed value for the constant. While multiple constants of the same type can be declared within a single constant declaration statement, all constants would be assigned the same fixed value.

Examples:
```
CONSTANT C6: std_logic_vector(2 DOWNTO 0) := "110";
CONSTANT Enable: std_logic := '0';
CONSTANT ClkPeriod: TIME := 20 ns;
```

FILE

```
FILE name : file_type;
FILE name : file_type IS file_name;
FILE name : file_type OPEN file_mode IS file_name;
```

A *file declaration statement* defines a file identifier that can be used for accessing information stored within a file. A *file* is a document located on the host computing system. A file declaration must at least define the file identifier and the file type. The predefined file type, *text*, and functions for accessing files are available in the package *std.textio.ALL*. A *text* file is a file that contains an arbitrary number of text (known as "ASCII") characters. The *text* file type is a very convenient file type to use as one can edit a text file within any text editor.

A file declaration can optionally specify the logical file name of the file — the logical file name is the name of the file on the host computing system and must be an expression of the predefined type *string*. If the file name is specified, an implicit call to the *file_open()* function will be called and the specified file will be opened with the default file access mode, *read_mode*. If the logical file name is specified and the desired access mode is not *read_mode*, the file declaration can also specify the file access mode. The *file access mode* can be either *read_mode*, *write_mode*, or *append_mode* depending on whether the file will be used for input or output. When a file is opened with *write_mode*, a new file will be created, replacing any previously existing file with the specified name. If a file is opened with *append_mode*, the file will be opened for output and any output to the file will be appended to the end of the existing file, or to a new file if the file did not previously exist.

Examples:

```
-- No implicit file_open
FILE vectorfile: text;

-- Implicit file_open with default
-- read_mode access
FILE infile: text IS "vectors.txt";

-- Explicit file_open with specified
-- write_mode access
FILE outfile: text OPEN write_mode IS "results";
```

SIGNAL

```
SIGNAL name: type;
SIGNAL name: type := default_value;
```

A *signal* is an object that holds, or stores, a value at a particular time. A *signal declaration* statement must specify the signal name and signal type, and can optionally define an initial value for the signal. Note that assigning an initial value to a signal is generally not synthesizable, but it can be useful for testbenches and simulation. Multiple signals of the same type can also be declared within a single signal declaration statement, where each signal name is separated by a comma.

Examples:

```
SIGNAL a: std_logic;
SIGNAL reg: std_logic_vector(1 DOWNTO 0) := "11";
SIGNAL x_s, y_s, F_s: std_logic;
```

Signals declarations must be included with the declarative part of an entity's architecture body.

Example:

```
ARCHITECTURE Circuit OF BeltWarn IS
    -- Declarations
    SIGNAL n1, n2: std_logic;
BEGIN
    -- Statements
END Circuit;
```

TYPE

A *type declaration* defines a new name that represents a set of possible values. Many different type declarations are possible within VHDL. The following includes details for a few common type declarations useful for digital design. All type declarations consist of two key items, the name of the type and the possible values an object of that type can represent.

Array

```
TYPE name IS ARRAY (constraint) OF element_type;
```

An *array* declaration defines an object that consists of a number of elements, all having the same subtype, and each being accessible using an index. An array declaration includes the new type name, an array constraint defining the size of the array, and the array element type that defines the type of element stored within the array. The array constraint can be used to define a *constrained* or *unconstrained* array.

A *constrained array* type declaration defines an array with a known number of elements within the array by specifying the size of the array as a discrete range enclosed by parentheses within the array constraint. All objects of a constrained array type will have exactly the same number of elements.

An *unconstrained array* declaration defines an array type that only specifies the type of elements within the array but not the range for the array index. An unconstrained array declaration must include within the array constraint the subtype for the array index followed by "*RANGE <>*", that specifies an undefined range. When declaring an object, such as a signal or variable, of an unconstrained array type, the object declaration must define the discrete range of the array within the declaration.

Examples:

```
-- Constrained array type declaration
TYPE regfile_type IS
    ARRAY (0 to 3) OF std_logic_vector(31 DOWNTO 0);
SIGNAL regfile: regfile_type;

-- Unconstrained array type declaration
TYPE Memory IS ARRAY (integer RANGE <>) OF
    std_logic_vector(8 DOWNTO 0);
SIGNAL DataMem: Memory (0 to 31);
```

Enumeration

```
TYPE name IS (identifier1, identifier1);
TYPE name IS (character1, character2);
```

An *enumeration* type declaration defines all possible values of the user defined type between the parentheses of the type declaration, where each distinct value is separated by a comma. A user defined enumerated type may either specify the values as multiple unique identifiers or as multiple unique characters.

Examples:

```
TYPE Statetype IS (S_Off, S_On1, S_On2, S_On3);
TYPE TriState IS ('0','1','Z');
```

Integer

```
TYPE name IS RANGE low_value TO high_value;
TYPE name IS RANGE high_value DOWNTO low_value;
```

An *integer* type declaration specifies an integer type and defines the *RANGE* of possible integers values the type can represent. Note that VHDL includes the pre-defined integer type, named *integer*, that is guaranteed to at least include the range –2147483647 to +2147483647, but may be larger depending on the implementation.

Example:

```
TYPE SmallInt IS RANGE 0 TO 16;
TYPE TwosComplementInt IS RANGE -256 TO 255;
TYPE Index IS RANGE 31 DOWNTO 0;
```

Subtype

```
SUBTYPE name IS restricted_type;
```

A *subtype declaration* declares a new subtype that is a restricted form of a previously defined type (or subtype). A subtype declaration includes the base type and a constraint that restricts the possible values of the base type that the newly created subtype may hold. The new type is a subtype in that it represents a subset of the possible values the base type can represent.

Examples:

```
SUBTYPE Statetype IS std_logic_vector(1 DOWNTO 0);

TYPE SmallInt IS RANGE 0 to 16;
SUBTYPE SmallerInt IS SmallInt RANGE 0 TO 8;
```

VARIABLE

```
VARIABLE name: type;
VARIABLE name: type := default_value;
```

A **variable declaration** declares a new storage item, and is similar to a signal except for the important distinction that a variable does not have a time aspect. Variables are defined within a process between the process declaration statement and the process begin statement, and can only be accessed within the process in which it is defined. Multiple variables of the same type can also be declared within a single variable declaration statement, where each variable name is separated by a comma. Note: revisions to VHDL allow for processes to share variables, but we do not discuss that advanced feature here.

Example:

```
PROCESS (A, B, Ci)
   VARIABLE A5, B5, S5:
      std_logic_vector(4 DOWNTO 0);
BEGIN
   A5 := '0' & A; B5 := '0' & B;
   S5 := A5 + B5 + Ci;
   S <= S5(3 DOWNTO 0);
   Co <= S5(4);
END PROCESS;
```

6.3 STATEMENTS

ASSERTION STATEMENT

```
ASSERT condition REPORT expression
     SEVERITY expression;
```

An **assertion statement** checks if a condition is true, reporting an error if the condition is false. An assertion statement includes the condition of the assertion, a *REPORT* clause, and a *SEVERITY* clause. The REPORT clause of the assertion statement is optional. If the REPORT clause is present, the clause must defines a literal or expression of type *string* that will be displayed if the condition of the assertion statement evaluates to false. If the REPORT clause is absent, the default report string "*Assertion violation*" will be printed.

Assert statements also allow for an optional *SEVERITY* clause included at the end of the assert statement. Possible SEVERITY value are *ERROR, WARNING,* and *NOTE,* with ERROR being the default value. The severity clause provides additional information to the simulator, allowing the simulator to decide how to report the error, which is specific to the simulator and can often be configured.

Example:

```
ASSERT a = '1';
ASSERT x_s = '0' REPORT "Reset failed";
ASSERT Q_s = X"000000FF"
    REPORT "Failed output enabled"
    SEVERITY warning;
```

ASSIGNMENT STATEMENT

Signal Assignment

signal_name <= *expression*;

A *signal assignment statement* assigns a value to a signal using the signal assignment operator, "<=". The left side of the assignment operator must be a signal. The right side of the signal assignment statement is an expression whose type is the same as the signal to which the expression result will be assigned. A signal assignment statement must end with a semicolon.

Examples:

```
F <= x AND y;
Q <= "0000";
Q <= (OTHERS=>'0');
I_reg <= I_reg + 1;
```

Concurrent Signal Assignment

signal_name <= *expression*;

A *concurrent signal assignment statement* is a signal assignment statement within an architecture body that assigns a value or expression to a signal. Unlike other signal assignment statements within a process, a concurrent signal assignment statement is essentially another process, executing concurrently with any other processes, and in fact is equivalent to a process that has the appropriate sensitivity list and a single signal assignment statement.

Example:

```
-- Architecture with concurrent signal
-- assignment statement
ARCHITECTURE Beh OF ShiftReg32 IS
```

```
        SIGNAL R: std_logic_vector(31 DOWNTO 0);
    BEGIN
        PROCESS (Clk)
        BEGIN
        -- Process statements
        END PROCESS;
        Q <= R;    -- Concurrent signal assignment
    END Beh;

    -- Process equivalent of the concurrent signal
    -- assignment statement "Q <= R;"
    PROCESS(R)
    BEGIN
        Q <= R;
    END PROCESS;
```

Variable Assignment

variable_name := **expression**;

A *variable assignment statement* assigns a value to a variable using the variable assignment operator, ":=". The left side of the variable assignment operator must be a variable. The right side of the variable assignment statement is an expression whose type is the same as the variable to which the expression result will be assgined. A variable assignment statement must end with a semicolon.

Examples:

```
    Sum := 0;
    S5 := A5 + B5 + Ci;
```

CASE STATEMENT

```
    CASE expression IS
        WHEN choice =>
            choice_statements
        WHEN choice =>
            choice_statements
        WHEN OTHERS =>
            choice_statements
    END CASE;
```

A *case statement* selects for execution one sequence of statements among several possible sequences of statements, based on the value of the case statement's expression, specified between the *CASE* and *IS* keywords of the statement. The case statement will evaluate the case expression and execute the sequence of statements within the choice whose value matches the value of the expression. Each choice within a case statement is defined by a **WHEN clause** that specifies the value of the choice between WHEN keyword and "=>" symbol followed by the sequence of statements to be executed when the choice is selected. The case expression must be a discrete type or an array type whose element base type is a character type, such as a *string*, *bit_vector*, or *std_logic_vector*.

A case statement must define all possible alternatives and defines a sequence of statements to execute for each option. In addition, a distinct value for the expression can only appear within one *WHEN* clause. Therefore, the case statement will execute exactly one sequence of statements within the corresponding choice. The case statement can include an **OTHERS** choice as the last alternative, specified as "*WHEN OTHERS =>*", within the case statement. The *OTHERS* choice corresponds to all other possible values of the case expression that are not defined in previous choices.

Example:

```
CASE Currstate IS
   WHEN S_Off =>
      x <= '0';
      IF (b = '0') THEN
         Nextstate <= S_Off;
      ELSE
         Nextstate <= S_On1;
      END IF;
   WHEN S_On1 =>
      x <= '1';
      Nextstate <= S_On2;
   WHEN S_On2 =>
      x <= '1';
      Nextstate <= S_On3;
   WHEN S_On3 =>
      x <= '1';
      Nextstate <= S_Off;
END CASE;

-- Case statement with WHEN OTHERS choice
CASE (sel) IS
   WHEN "00" =>
      d <= i0;
   WHEN "01" =>
```

```
        d <= i1;
   WHEN "10" =>
        d <= i2;
   WHEN "11" =>
        d <= i3;
   WHEN OTHERS =>
        d <= 'Z';
END CASE;
```

COMPONENT INSTANTIATION

```
instance_name: component_type
   port_map
   generic_map;
```

A *component instantiation* statement creates a single instance of a component in a circuit, and describes how that instance connects with the circuit signals. The component instantiation statement specifies a unique name for the component instance, the type of component being instantiated, a port map, and a generic map.

Port Map

```
PORT MAP (signal, signal);
PORT MAP (port => signal, port => signal);
```

The *port map* part of a component instantiation statement connects the component instance's ports to signals within the circuit. A *positional* port map has a list of signals defined within parentheses, where each signal in the list connects to a port of the component according to the order of ports in the component declaration. A *named* port map explicitly maps the instance's ports by name to signals within circuit signals. In a named port map, the ordering of the items within the port map does not matter.

Examples:

```
-- Component instantiation with positional
-- port map
CompToTest: Add4 PORT MAP (A_s, B_s, S_s);

-- Component instantiation with named port map
CompToTest: Add4 PORT MAP (S=>S_s, A=>A_s, B=>B_s);
```

Generic Map

```
GENERIC MAP (value, value);
GENERIC MAP (generic => value, generic => value);
```

The *generic map* part of a component instantiation statement associates values with component instance's generics. A *positional* generic map has a list of values within parentheses, where each value in the list defines the value of the a generic of the component according to the order of generics in the component declaration. A *named* generic map explicitly maps the instance's generics by name to values being associated with those generics. A generic map can assign to the generics of a component instance the generic values of the enclosing entity declaration, as the generics of the entity are generic constants that will be statically defined within a component instantiation of the enclosing entity.

Example:

```
-- Component declaration with a generic
COMPONENT Adder IS
    GENERIC (Width: integer := 4);
    PORT (A: IN std_logic_vector(Width-1 DOWNTO 0);
          B: IN std_logic_vector(Width-1 DOWNTO 0);
          S: OUT std_logic_vector(Width-1 DOWNTO 0));
END COMPONENT;

-- Component instantiation with named port map
-- and named generic map
CompToTest: Adder
    PORT MAP (S=>S_s, A=>A_s, B=>B_s)
    GENERIC MAP (Width=>32);
```

IF STATEMENT

```
IF condition THEN
    if_statements
ELSIF condition THEN
    elsif_statements
ELSE
    else_statements
END IF;
```

An *IF statement* selects for execution one or none of the defined sequences of statements based on the evaluation of the conditions defined within the various parts of the IF statement. The IF statement can include multiple parts - a single IF part, zero or more ELSIF parts, and single final ELSE part. The IF statement begins by evaluating the condition within the IF part, specified between the IF and THEN keywords of the IF statement. If this condition evaluates to true, then the statements following the THEN keyword are executed, and the remaining parts of the IF statement will be skipped. If the IF condition instead evaluates to false, the statements following the THEN are skipped, and instead the following ELSIF of ELSE part of the IF statement are evaluated. An IF statement can have one or more ELSIF parts to handle multiple possible conditions. The first ELSIF part whose condition evaluates to true will have its statements executed, and the remaining parts of the IF statement will be skipped. If no conditions within the IF statement evaluate to true and an ELSE part is defined, the statements within the ELSE part will be executed. An IF statement always ends with *"END IF;"*, regardless of whether or not an ELSE part exists. The conditions defined within an IF statement must be specified as Boolean expression.

Examples:

```
-- IF statement
IF (ld = '1') THEN
    Q <= I;
END IF;


-- IF-ELSE statement
IF (Cnt_s = '1') THEN
    CntNext <= "10";
ELSE
    CntNext <= Cnt - "01";
END IF;


-- IF-ELSIF-ELSE statement
IF (A < B) THEN
    Gt<='0'; Eq<='0'; Lt<='1';
ELSIF (A > B) THEN
    Gt<='1'; Eq<='0'; Lt<='0';
ELSE
    Gt<='0'; Eq<='1'; Lt<='0';
END IF;
```

LOOP STATEMENT

A *loop statement* defines a sequence of statements that will be executed repeatedly for some number of times. The loop statement defines the loop type, which can be either *FOR* or *WHILE*, the loop parameter that controls how many times the loop will be executed, and the sequence of statements to be executed during each loop iteration.

FOR Loop

```
FOR identifier IN discrete_range LOOP
    loop_statements
END LOOP;
```

A *FOR loop* is a loop that executes a discrete number of times as specified by the loop parameter. The *loop parameter* defines an identifier for the loop index and a discrete range of values over which the loop will iterate. The FOR loop executes the loop statements for the specified number of times. During each iteration of the loop, the loop index will successively be assigned the values within the defined range. The loop range of a FOR loop is inclusive, meaning that the loop will execute once for each distinct value defined within the range. For example, a loop defined as "*FOR index IN 0 TO 30 LOOP*" will execute a total of 31 times. The sequence of statements that will be executed during each loop iteration is defined within the loop body between the loop declaration and the "*END LOOP;*" statement.

Examples:

```
FOR index IN 0 TO 30 LOOP
    R(index) <= R(index+1);
END LOOP;

FOR i IN inputline'RANGE LOOP
    read(inputline, inputbit);
    IF inputbit = '1' THEN
        Shr_in_s <= '1';
    ELSE
        Shr_in_s <= '0';
    END IF;
END LOOP;
```

WHILE Loop

```
WHILE condition LOOP
    loop_statements
END LOOP;
```

A *WHILE loop* is a loop that continues to execute a sequence of statements as long as the loop's condition evaluates to true. The *loop condition* is a Boolean expression that will be evaluated before each execution of the loop's statements. If the condition evaluates to true, the loop's statement will be executed. If the loop condition evaluates to false, the loop's execution is complete. The sequence of statements that will be executed during each loop iteration is defined within the loop body before the *"END LOOP;"* statement.

Example:

```
WHILE (Go='0') LOOP
END LOOP;

WHILE (NOT endfile(vectorfile)) LOOP
    -- File IO statements
END LOOP;
```

PROCESS

```
process_label:
PROCESS(sensitivity_list)
    declarative_part
BEGIN
    statements_part
END PROCESS process_label;
```

A *process* statement defines a sequence of statements that are repeatedly executed. A process statement represents one method of describing an entity's behavior within the entity's architecture body. A process statement defines the process' sensitivity list, declarative part, and statements part. The *sensitivity list* of a process lists the signals, including ports, of the design on which the process is sensitive. A process that specifies a sensitivity list will only execute its statements if the value of one the items within the sensitivity list changes. The process' declarative part incudes declarations of items that are available within the process and may include variables, file, constant, and type declarations, among others. The process' statements part defines the sequence of statements that will be repeatedly executed within the process.

A process may also include an optional process label that defines a name for the process. A process label is an identifier specified at the beginning of the process declaration followed by a colon preceding the *PROCESS* keyword. When a process label is specified, the process label should also be specified at the end the process statement after *"END PROCESS"* but before the final semicolon, as in the example, *"END PROCESS VectorProcess;"*.

Examples:

```
-- Process with sensitivity list
PROCESS(x, y)
BEGIN
    F <= x AND y;
END PROCESS;

-- Process without sensitivity but
-- with a process label
ClkProcess: PROCESS
BEGIN
    Clk_s <= '0';
    WAIT FOR 10 NS;
    Clk_s <= '1';
    WAIT FOR 10 NS;
END PROCESS ClkProcess;
```

WAIT STATEMENT

```
WAIT ON sensitivity_list
    UNTIL condition
    FOR time_expression;
```

A *wait statement* in a process tells the simulator to suspend execution of the process. A wait statement consists of several parts, including a sensitivity list, condition clause, and timeout clause. The wait statement's *sensitivity list* defines the signals to which the wait statement is sensitive. Whenever the value of a signal within the sensitivity list changes, the process will evaluate the wait statements *condition clause* to determine if the process should still be suspended by the wait statement. The condition clause of a wait statement defines a Boolean expression following the *UNTIL* keyword. If the value of the condition evaluates to true, the process will resume execution. If the condition evaluates to false, the process will be suspended again until a signal within the sensitivity list changes. If a sensitivity list is not specified, the sensitivity list will be automatically be constructed from the condition clause. If the condition clause is not specified, the default condition "UNTIL true" is assumed.

A wait statement can also tell the simulator how long to wait before resuming execution by using a *timeout clause* that defines the maximum amount of time the process should wait before executing again. The timeout clause is defined as a time value following the *FOR* keyword. For example, the timeout clause "*FOR 10 ns*" specifies that the process execution should only be suspended for a maximum of 10 ns, even if no signals within the wait statement's sensitivity list change or the condition clause does not evaluate to true.

The statement *"WAIT;"* defines a wait statement without a sensitivity list, condition clause, or timeout clause, and will permanently suspend the execution of the process.

Examples:

```
WAIT; -- Will wait forever
WAIT UNTIL Clk_s='1' AND Clk_s'EVENT;
WAIT FOR 10 ns;
WAIT ON S;
WAIT ON S UNTIL S='0' FOR 10 ns;
```

6.4 OPERATORS

VHDL defines arithmetic, logical, relational, and other operators for the predefined types, *bit*, *boolean*, and *integer*. However, these same operators, or subset of operators, are typically defined for additional types, such as *std_logic*, *std_logic_vector*, *signed*, and *unsigned*, within the packages that define the types.

ARITHMETIC

Arithmetic operators for the predefined *integer* type including addition, "+", subtraction, "-", concatenation "&", multiplication, "*", division, "/", modulus, *MOD*, remainder, *REM*, absolute value, *ABS*, exponentiation, "**", and the sign operators identity, "+", and negation, "-". Note that the negation and subtraction operators, as well as the addition and identity operators, both utilize the same symbol for the operator. Because the negate operator is a unary operator and has higher precedence, distinguishing between the two operators within a VHDL description is straightforward.

All of these operators can be generally classified as arithmetic operators. However, VHDL further classifies theses operators into addition, sign, multiplication, and miscellaneous operators, in order to establish the operator precedence discussed in a latter section.

Examples:

```
S <= A + B;
I_reg <= I_reg - 1;
mulout <= a * b;
A <= -B;
```

Concatenation

The concatenation operator, "&", is classified as an arithmetic operator, although the concatenation operator can be also used to concatenate *bit_vector*, *std_logic_vector*, *unsigned*, and *signed* types. The concatenation operator combines its left and right bit vectors into one larger vector value. The concatenation operator can also be used to combine two single bit items, such as *bit* or *std_logic*, into a multi-bit vector, such as *bit_vector* or *std_logic_vector*.

Examples:

```
A5 <= '0' & A;
B5 := B(3) & B;
```

LOGICAL

The logical operators, *NOT, AND, OR, XOR, NAND, NOR, XNOR* are defined for the predefined types, *bit, boolean,* and *bit_vector.* The logical operators are also defined for *std_logic* and *std_logic_vector* within the package *ieee.std_logic_1164.ALL.* While the NOT operator is considered a logical operator, NOT has a higher precedence than the other logical operators.

Examples:

```
F <= x AND y;
w <= k AND p AND NOT(s);
F <= NOT x;
```

RELATIONAL

The relational operators allow us to compare the operands to test for equality, "=", inequality, "/=", as well as the ordering of the operands including comparisons for less than, "<", less than or equal, "<=", greater than, ">", and greater than or equal, ">=". The result of all relational operators is a Boolean value of the predefined type *boolean.*

Examples:

```
ASSERT Q_s = X"FFFF0000";
WAIT UNTIL Clk_s='1' AND Clk_s'EVENT;

-- IF-ELSIF-ELSE statement using relational
-- operators in the IF and ELSIF conditions
IF (A < B) THEN
```

```
    Gt<='0'; Eq<='0'; Lt<='1';
ELSIF (A > B) THEN
    Gt<='1'; Eq<='0'; Lt<='0';
ELSE
    Gt<='0'; Eq<='1'; Lt<='0';
END IF;
```

SHIFT

The shift, and rotate, operators are defined for vectors of the predefined types *bit* or *boolean*, such as a *bit_vector*. The shift operators include shift left logical, *SLL*, shift right logical, *SRL*, shift left arithmetic, *SLA*, shift right arithmetic, *SRA*, rotate left, *ROL*, and rotate right, *ROR*. The left operand of a shift operation must specify a vector whose value will be shifted. The right operand of a shift operation specifies an *integer* expression defining the number of bit positions to shift the vector.

Examples:

```
R <= R_in SRL 2;
Reg <= Reg ROR 8;
```

OPERATOR PRECEDENCE

The operator precedence in VHDL is defined by classifying operators into several precedence levels. All operators within the same level have the same precedence and are evaluated from left to right. The following lists the VHDL precedence levels from highest to lowest precedence and the operators defines within each precedence level.

- Miscellaneous: *NOT, ABS, ***
- Multiplication: **, /, MOD, REM*
- Sign: +, -
- Addition: +, -, &
- Shift: *SLL, SRL, SLA, SRA, ROL, ROR*
- Relational: =, /=, <, <=, >, >=
- Logical: *AND, OR, XOR, NAND, NOR, XNOR*

6.5 COMMON DATA TYPES

BIT

```
TYPE bit IS ('0','1');
```

The *bit* type is a predefined type in VHDL that can represent the logic values of *'0'* and *'1'*.

BIT_VECTOR

```
TYPE bit_vector IS ARRAY (natural RANGE <>) OF bit;
```

The *bit_vector* type is a predefined type in VHDL that defines a collection of *bits* as an unconstrained array. A declaration of a signal or variable of type *bit_vector* must specify the numbering and order of the bits within the vector, as the *bit_vector* type declaration does not specify this information. To access an individual bit of a vector, the bit position must be specified within parentheses following the vector name. For example, the statement "$Q(2) <= I(1);$" would assign bit 1 of I to bit 2 of the Q.

Assigning all bits of a *bit_vector* to the same value can be accomplished using the "*OTHERS*" notation. For example, the statement "$R <= (OTHERS=>'0');$" assigns *0*s to all bits of the vector R, essentially having the same behavior as the assignment statement "$R <= X"00000000";$", where R is a 32 bit vector. The notation is a bit awkward due to actually being usable in a more general scenario, but the notation is commonly used to set all bits of a vector to a particular value as used here. This notation is not only somewhat shorter, but is also independent of the number of bits in the vector.

Example:

```
-- bit_vector signal declaration
SIGNAL A: bit_vector(3 DOWNTO 0);

-- bit_vector signal assignment
A <= "0000";
A <= X"0";
A(0) <= '0';
A <= (OTHERS=>'1');
```

BOOLEAN

```
TYPE boolean IS (false, true);
```

The *boolean* type is a predefined type in VHDL that can represent the logical values of *true* and *false*

STD_LOGIC

The *std_logic* type is declared in the *ieee.std_logic_1164.ALL* package and can represent the many possible values a digital signal can have in a hardware circuit. The *std_logic* type can represent the logic values *'0'* and *'1'* along with *'U'* to represent an uninitialized signal, *'X'* to represents an unknown value, *'Z'* to represent high impedance, *'-'* to represent a don't care, *'L'* to represent a weak signal that should be *'0'*, *'H'* to represent a weak signal that should be *'1'*, and *'W'* to represent a weak signal for which the value cannot be determined.

Example:

```
-- Package required to use std_logic
LIBRARY ieee;
USE ieee.std_logic_1164.ALL;

-- std_logic signal declaration
SIGNAL s0: std_logic;

-- std_logic signal assignment
s0 <= '0';
s0 <= '1';
s0 <= a XOR '1';
```

STD_LOGIC_VECTOR

The *std_logic_vector* type is a collection of bits, where each bit is defined as a *std_logic*. A declaration of a signal or variable of type *std_logic_vector* must specify the numbering and order of the bits within the vector. To access an individual bit of a vector, the bit position must be specified within parentheses following the vector name. Similar to a *bit_vector*, to access an individual bit of a *std_logic_vector*, the bit position must be specified within parentheses following the vector name, e.g., the statement "*Q(2) <= I(1);*" would assign bit 1 of *I* to bit 2 of the *Q*.

Assigning all bits of a *std_logic_vector* to the same value can be accomplished using the "***OTHERS***" notation. For example, the statement "*R <= (OTH­ERS=>'0');*" assigns *0*s to all bits of the vector *R*, essentially having the same behavior as the assignment statement "*R* <= *X"00000000";*", where *R* is a 32 bit vector. The notation is a bit awkward due to actually being usable in a more general scenario, but the notation is commonly used to set all bits of a vector to a particular value, as is done above. This notation is not only somewhat shorter, but is also independent of the number of bits in the vector.

Example:

```
-- Package required to utilize std_logic
-- and std_logic_vector
LIBRARY ieee;
USE ieee.std_logic_1164.ALL;

-- std_logic_vector signal declaration
SIGNAL A: std_logic_vector(3 DOWNTO 0);

-- std_logic signal assignment
A <= "0111";
A <= "ZZZZ";
A <= X"A";
A(0) <= 'Z';
A<= (OTHERS=>'Z');
```

SIGNED AND UNSIGNED

Several options existing for defining signed and unsigned numbers within a VHDL description. The following provides descriptions for three options for specifying signed and unsigned numbers, although other options may exist.

ieee.std_logic_unsigned and ieee.std_logic_signed

The package *ieee.std_logic_unsigned.ALL* defines arithmetic operations "+", "-", "*", and "/" (add, subtract, multiply, and divide), and relational operations "<", "<=", "=", "/=", ">=", and ">", for *std_logic_vector* types, assuming that all *std_logic_vector* items are unsigned binary numbers. Alternatively, the package *ieee.std_logic_signed.ALL* defines those same arithmetic and relational operations assuming that all *std_logic_vector* items are two's complement (signed) numbers. An architecture can only use one of those two packages, *ieee.std_logic_signed.ALL* or *ieee.std_logic_unsigned.ALL*, but can not use both. Otherwise, it would not be clear whether operators like "+" should perform signed or unsigned operations.

Example:

```
-- Package required to treat all std_logic_vectors
```

```
-- as unsigned numbers
USE ieee.std_logic_1164.ALL;
USE ieee.std_logic_unsigned.ALL;

-- Arithmetic and relational operators
-- will perform unsigned calculation
S <= A + B;
```

ieee.std_logic_arith

If both signed and unsigned numbers are required within the same architecture, one possible solution is to use the package *ieee.std_logic_arith.ALL*, which includes two logic vector types named *signed* and *unsigned*, and also defines arithmetic operations "+", "-", "*", and "/" (add, subtract, multiply, and divide), and relational operations "<", "<=", "=", "/=", ">=", and ">"operators for any combination of *unsigned* and *signed* operands. By using this package, both *signed* and *unsigned* items can be explicitly declared within a design.

Example:

```
-- Packages required to include unsigned and
-- signed in same architecture
USE ieee.std_logic_1164.ALL;
USE ieee.std_logic_arith.ALL;

SIGNAL A_s: unsigned(3 DOWNTO 0);
SIGNAL B_s: signed(3 DOWNTO 0);
```

ieee.numeric_std

The packages *ieee.std_logic_unsigned.ALL*, *ieee.std_logic_signed.ALL*, and *ieee.std_logic_arith.ALL* were originally developed by a EDA tool vendor to define *signed* and *unsigned* types and the associated arithmetic and relational operators. While most simulation and synthesis tools support these packages, the packages are not officially standardized and may exhibit slight differences between implementations. An extension to the VHDL standard defines the package *ieee.numeric_std.ALL,* which also includes two logic vector types named *signed* and *unsigned*, and defines the operators "+", "-", "*", "<", "<=", "=", "/=", ">=", and ">" for several combinations of *unsigned* and *signed* operands.

Example:

```
-- Package required to include unsigned and signed
-- in same architecture
USE ieee.std_logic_1164.ALL;
```

```
USE ieee.numeric_std.ALL;

SIGNAL A_s: unsigned(3 DOWNTO 0);
SIGNAL B_s: signed(3 DOWNTO 0);
```

Index

Symbols

"&"

    See concatenation operator

"+"

    See addition operator

":="

    See variable assignment operator

"<="

    See signal assignment operator

"--"

    See comment

'Z'

    See high impedance

A